T0090852

WHAT YOU SHOULD KNOW ABOUT

يهملكن

REV. THEODORE BOWERS

iUniverse®

WHAT YOU SHOULD KNOW ABOUT ISLAM

iUniverse books may be ordered through booksellers or by contacting:

iUniverse
1663 Liberty Drive
Bloomington, IN 47403
www.iuniverse.com
844-349-9409

ISBN: 978-1-5320-9746-1 (sc)
ISBN: 978-1-5320-9747-8 (e)

Print information available on the last page.

iUniverse rev. date: 02/25/2021

CONTENTS

ACKNOWLEDGEMENTS

This book is dedicated to my family, friends, and mentors who provided me with guidance, encouragement, and assistance in writing this book. My daughter Marianne Bowers provided composing assistance; my son Jeffrey Bowers sketched the illustrations; my friend Richard Busch provided practical suggestions; my friend Donna Lebeduik provided proofing; and my Kuwaiti friend, whose name I cannot provide in order to protect him from any repercussions, provided me with information about the culture of the Arabian Peninsula.

I also wish to acknowledge the authors Ben Ferguson and Rev. Craig Loewen who offered suggestions and advice regarding the publication of my book.

I also want to acknowledge my seminary professors at Winebrenner Theological Seminary who, many years ago, challenged me and provided me with the tools and inspiration to reach for higher goals:

Dr. Gale Ritz, former President and Old Testament scholar who inspired me through his teaching of the Psalms and themes of the Old Testament;

Dr. Richard Kern, professor of Church History who provided me with the opportunity to explore new avenues of service;

Dr. Clair Harman, professor of New Testament who was patient with me and helped me to conduct critical analysis.

And most of all, to my wife who, through the many years of our marriage, was patient and accepted my decisions while always offering positive suggestions and advice.

Rev. Theodore E. Bowers

CDR, CHC, USN, ret

PREFACE

My purpose for writing this book is to share my belief regarding the religion of Islam. This book is not a technical treatise. I rely on the research and theories of a number of authors and scholars. I want the reader to learn some important history and teachings of Islam and how they compare and/or contrast with the teachings of Judaism and Christianity. My secondary purpose is to give the reader a brief overview of the beginnings of Islam as well as how and why it is affecting our world today.

One of my basic tenets is that Islam is a religious/political phenomenon that incorporated the religious teachings of both Judaism and Christianity, combined with the culture and traditions of the Arabian Peninsula. Its prophet, Muhammad, had experienced the teachings of Christianity and Judaism and the concept of monotheism. His later followers developed an institutionalized system of religious beliefs, attitudes, and practices along with a political system of laws and regulations based on what they believed Muhammad had intended.

Islam's prophet—or "apostle" or "messenger"—needs to be demythologized by examining his background, teachings, and actions, along with the culture of Arabia prior to and during his lifetime. I believe that Islam is a system based on works and fanatical belief, not faith. However, I will begin by providing a glimpse of ancient Israel and the Hebrew people because they predate Islam by at least two millennia. From the beginnings of the Hebrew people, they worshiped one God but were constantly chastised by God and His prophets when they drifted into the worship of the gods of their neighbors or when difficult times arose.

We will examine Islam in the context of the Middle East from the 2nd millennium BC to the seventh century AD, as well as how it interfaced with Judaism and Christianity throughout the centuries, particularly from the Crusades to modern-day radicalism.

One final observation: After exploring the writings of several authors and scholars, I have come to the conclusion that much of the information of the historical personage of Muhammad, including his revelations, his life, and his teachings, are not trustworthy. Several modern scholars believe that many of the traditions surrounding Muhammad's life were fabrications created long after his death in an attempt to give meaning to the Koran. However, I don't agree with those scholars who doubt the existence of the prophet named Muhammad.

CHAPTER 1

BEGINNING WITH ABRAHAM

Our story begins with the Patriarch Abraham, from whom Judaism, Christianity, and Islam derive their religious heritage.*(1)* They all trace their history back to God's covenant with Abram (Abraham). Islam, Judaism, and Christianity are separated by a disagreement regarding *who* are the inheritors of that covenant.

The Call of Abram

Sometime after 2000 BC, Terah, the father of Abram, decided to leave Ur of the Chaldees. (Ur was the wealthiest city of the Sumerian region.) The southern region of Sumer later became part of the Babylonian Empire and, today, modern Iraq and Kuwait. Terah took with him his son Abram and his wife Sarai, Nahor his other son, and Lot, a grandson whose father was deceased. His destination was the land of Canaan. However, they made it as far as Haran, which today is in southeastern Turkey, and settled there.

God's Covenant to Abram (Abraham): It was in Haran where Abram received his first call from God:

> *Leave your country, your people and your father's household and go to the land I will show you. I will make you a great nation and I will bless you; I will*

> *make your name great, and you will be a blessing. I will bless you, and whoever curses you I will curse; and all peoples on earth will be blessed through you. So Abram left, as the Lord told him; and Lot went with him . . . and they set out for the land of Canaan, and they arrived there. (2)*

The word of the Lord came to Abram in a vision:

> *Do not be afraid, Abram. I am your shield, your reward will be very great. (3)*

Abram was upset:

> *You have given me no children; so a servant in my household will be my heir. (4)*

The Lord spoke to him:

> *This man will not be your heir, but a son coming from your own body will be your heir. (5)*

There was a famine in Canaan, so Abram and Sarai traveled to Egypt. Because of Sarai's beauty, Abram was afraid the Egyptians would kill him so they could have her. He decided to claim that she was his sister. The Pharaoh took her into his palace to add to his harem. The Pharaoh gave Abram sheep, cattle, donkeys, and servants. One of the servants given to Abram was Hagar, who, in turn, later became Sarai's maidservant. *(5)* Serious diseases affected Pharaoh's household because Sarai was Abram's wife. When Pharaoh discovered Sarai was Abram's wife, he summoned Abram, reprimanded him, and told him "Here is your wife. Take her and go!" Abram went back to Canaan wealthier that when he had left.

Sarai was barren and offered her Egyptian servant Hagar to Abram to have his children. Abram agreed. Abram took Hagar as a wife, and she became pregnant. Hagar then began to despise Sarai. Sarai complained to Abram, and Abram told her to do with her whatever way she thought best. And so Sarai mistreated Hagar, and Hagar fled to the desert. An angel of the Lord told Hagar to go back and submit to her mistress. The angel then made this covenant (promise) to Hagar:

> *I will so increase your descendants that they will be too numerous to count. . . . You are now with child and you will have a son. You shall name him Ishmael, for the Lord has heard of your misery. He will be a wild donkey of a man; his hand will be against everyone and everyone's hand against him, and he will live in hostility toward all his brothers. (6)*

What a Covenant—prophecy! And how true this was in the past and even more so in today's world affairs!

God Reaffirms His Covenant with Abram

God reaffirms His Covenant with Abram and renames him *Abraham*, *". . . . for I have made you a father of many nations."(7)* God also give Sarai a new name, *Sarah. "I will bless her so that she will be the mother of nations; kings of peoples will come from her." (8)*

Since Sarah was ninety years old and past the age of childbearing, Abraham fell down laughing. Then God said to Abraham:

> *Yes, but your wife Sarah will bear you a son, and you will call him Isaac. I will establish my covenant for his descendants after him. And as for Ishmael, I have heard you: I will surely bless him; I will make him fruitful and will greatly increase his numbers. He will be the father of twelve rulers, and I will make him into a great nation. But my covenant I*

> **will establish with Isaac, whom Sarah will bear to
> you by this time next year. (9)**

Hagar and Ishmael: The eldest son traditionally inherited all the assets of his father, according to the custom of the Sumerian culture of which both the Israelites and the Arabians were descendants.

Sarah did bear a son and called him Isaac. Sarah went to Abraham and requested that he send away Hagar and her son Ishmael, ". . . *for that slave woman's son will never share in the inheritance with my son Isaac."(10)* Abraham was distressed by this request, but God affirmed to him that Ishmael would become a nation because of his father. And so, Abraham sent Hagar and Ishmael off into the desert (Arabia).

The Scriptures refer to Ishmael's descendants as "Ishmaelites." Some of the Ishmaelites were traders of spice, balm, and myrrh. Abraham's grandson Jacob, who inherited God's promise to Abraham, had twelve sons. Jacob's sons threw their brother Joseph into a pit to die. They then saw an Ishmaelite camel caravan traveling to Egypt and decided to sell Joseph to the Ishmaelites for twenty shekels of silver. The Ishmaelites then, in turn, sold Joseph to one of Pharaoh's officials, Potiphar. *(11)* It is believed that the Ishmaelites were probably the desert tribes who harassed the Israelites during the times of the Judges but were not mentioned in the Scriptures after the time of King David.

The interpretation of God's Covenant from the Jewish Torah and the Christian Old Testament is what divides the Jews and Christians from Islam. Islam teaches that Ishmael (Abraham's oldest son) was the son of God's Covenant with Abraham and therefore, Ishmael and his descendants are the true inheritors of the seed of God's Covenant (Promise). The 7th century AD "prophet" Mohammad based his teaching on this premise.

The Koran (**Qur'an**), Islam's sacred scriptures, reinterprets the Judeo-Christian scriptures thousands of years after they were recorded in the

Torah to claim that to follow the teachings, revelations, and actions of Mohammad is the correct interpretation of the Covenant God made with Abraham. Islam claims that the Jewish scriptures are corrupt and that their writers purposely distorted the truth. Islam believes that the Koran, which was supposedly given over a period of time to Mohammad, is the literal word of God . . . and that God apparently speaks in Arabic and hears only Arabic. (For more on the Koran and the other Islamic writings, see Chapter 5.)

THE STORY OF ISHMAEL ACCORDING TO THE KORAN AND ISLAMIC TRADITION

In the teachings of Islam, because Ishmael is the oldest son of Abraham, he is the one whom Abraham was told to sacrifice. Abraham tells Ishmael of Allah's **(Islam's name for God)** command, and Ishmael encourages Abraham to listen to Allah because he is willing to be sacrificed. (He "*surrenders*" his will to Allah.) *(12)*

Because of Ishmael's willingness to be sacrificed, his actions have become the model of hospitality and obedience. Ishmael is, thus, the model of surrendering one's will to Allah, the demand for all Muslims. According to the Koran, as Abraham is about to sacrifice Ishmael, either the knife is turned over in his hand or copper appears on Ishmael's body and prevents his death. Allah tells Abraham that he has fulfilled the obligation. Abraham is then told to perform a "great Sacrifice." *(13)* Ishmael is considered a prophet of Allah (apostle) and is praised in the Koran for being patient, good, obedient, and righteous. *(14)*

Abraham then took Hagar and Ishmael to the Arabian Desert to the Valley of Bakkah, based on Allah's commands. There was literally no life there—not even water. Abraham was commanded by Allah to build a "House of Worship" called the Kaaba **(Arabic for "cube," the shape of the building)**. The Koran contains several verses regarding the origin of the Kaaba. It states that the Kaaba was the first House of

Worship and that it was built or rebuilt by Abraham (Arabic: "*Ibrahim*") on God's instructions.

> *Verily, the first House (of worship) appointed for mankind was that at Bakkah (Mecca), full of blessing, and guidance for mankind. (15)*
>
> *Behold! We gave the site, to Ibrahim, of the (Sacred) House, (saying): "Associate not anything (in worship) with Me; and sanctify My House for those who compass it round, or stand up, or bow, or prostrate themselves (therein in prayer)." (16)*
>
> *And remember Ibrahim and Ishmael raised the foundations of the House (With this prayer): "Our Lord! Accept (this service) from us: For Thou art the All-Hearing, the All-knowing." (17)*

While Abraham was building this cubical building *(18)* for worship, an angel brought to him the Black Stone, which he placed in the eastern corner of the structure. Another stone was the "Station of Abraham,*(19)* where Abraham stood for elevation while building the structure. The Black Stone and the Station of Abraham stone are believed by Muslims to be the only remnant of the original structure made by Abraham because the remaining structure was demolished and rebuilt several times over the course of history for maintenance purposes. After the construction was complete, God ordered the descendants of Ishmael to perform an annual pilgrimage, the *Hajj*, followed by the sacrifice of cattle. The vicinity of the shrine was also made a sanctuary where bloodshed and war were forbidden.

After the worship building was rebuilt, Abraham left Hagar and his son Ishmael and journeyed back to Canaan. Hagar and Ishmael became very thirsty after the water they brought with them for the journey was gone. Hagar prayed to Allah to provide water for them. Hagar then started to desperately run back and forth to search for water. Allah then caused Ishmael to strike his feet against the sand, and water gushed up, and they were saved. They then began to trade water with the tribes and caravans for food and other needs. The well became known as the famous Well of Zamzam, an important part of the experience of the Hajj.

After roaming the wilderness for some time, Ishmael and his mother settled in the Desert of Paran, where he became an expert in archery. Eventually, his mother found him a wife from the land of Egypt. They had twelve sons who each became tribal chiefs throughout the regions from Havilah to Shur (from Assyria to the border of Egypt). His sons were:

1. **Nebaioth**: (means "First-born" or "First Fruit" in Arabic)
2. **Kedar**: father of the Qedarites, a northern Arab tribe that controlled the area between the Persian Gulf and the Sinai Peninsula. According to tradition, he is the ancestor of the Quraysh tribe, and thus of the Islamic prophet, Muhammad.
3. **Adbeel**: established a tribe in northwest Arabia.
4. **Mibsam**: (means "Smiley" in Arabic)
5. **Mishma**: (means "Obeyed" in Arabic)
6. **Dumah**: (means "Sand-Hill" in Arabi
7. **Massa**: (means "Night Fall" in Arabic) father of a nomadic tribe that inhabited the Arabian desert in Babylonia.
8. **Hadad**: (means "The Rolling-Stone" in Arabic)
9. **Tema**: (means "The Good News" or "The Right Hand Man" in Arabic)
10. **Jetur**: (means "Revolt" or "Rebel" in Arabic)
11. **Naphish**: (means "Genuine" or "Precious" in Arabic)
12. **Kedemah**: (means "The Front Man" or "Scout" in Arabic)

Ishmael also had one known daughter, Mahalath or Basemath, the third wife of Esau, Isaac's firstborn son. Ishmael appeared with Isaac at the burial of Abraham. Ishmael died at the age of 137. Islamic tradition states that he was buried in Mecca, somewhere near the Kaaba.

Comment: *If some of the events don't sound consistent, there is conflicting information in the Koran and also in the other sacred Islamic writings. Islamic jurists also don't always agree on which information in the sacred writings is authentic and which is not.*

---

(1) Judaism, Christianity, and Islam begin with the Creation story, but for historical purposes, I will begin with Abraham.
(2) Genesis 12:1–5 (New International Version)
(3) Genesis 15:1 (NIV)
(4) Genesis 15:3 (NIV)
(5) Genesis 15:4 (NIV)
(6) Genesis 16:11-12 (NIV)
(7) Genesis 17:5 (NIV)
(8) Genesis 17:16 (NIV)
(9) Genesis 17:19-21 (NIV)
(10) Genesis 21:10 (NIV)
(11) Genesis 37:25-28; 39:1 (NIV)
(12) The word Islam means "to surrender".
(13) Once a year, Muslims slaughter an animal to commemorate Abraham's sacrifice in the Feast of Eied-al-Adha to be reminded that self-denial is the way of Allah.
(14) Koran 19: 54-55
(15) Koran 3:96
(16) Koran 22:26
(17) Koran 2:127
(18) Kaaba: Arabic for "cube"
(19) Maqam-e-Ibrahim: "the Station of Abraham"

CHAPTER 2

PRE-ISLAMIC ARABIA

(Prior to 600 AD)

Most of the people of the Middle East belong to the same family, the **Semitic Family**—members of any of the various ancient and modern peoples originating in Mesopotamia, including Arabs, Hebrews, Canaanites, Phoenicians, and Akkadians. The Semites traced their common descent to **Shem** (son of Noah) and spoke one of the Semitic languages. Traditionally, the Semitic people were nomadic by nature.

- Some settled around oases and developed a more urban life and often these oases developed into commercial centers for trade and industry
- Some settled near the fertile valleys of the Tigris and Euphrates Rivers, following a more agrarian lifestyle
- Many followed the nomadic life of herdsmen called **Bedouins**

There were two types of Bedouins. One type lived off herds, raiding other tribes, and receiving protection bounty; the other type was more an urban oasis culture.

There were certain cultural customs that were common among the various Semitic people:

- Rite of circumcision
- Laws
- Beards and mustaches
- Clothing
- Marriage and polygamy
- Tribes and Clans
- Desert hospitality

The tribes were organized into closely knit blood ties with a stern code of the law of retribution or blood revenge; polytheism with invisible spirits playing a central role; and the claim that their ancestral "father" was Abraham through his son Ishmael. (This was not true of the Jewish and Christian tribes who traced their claim of their ancestral father to Abraham through his son ***Isaac***.)

The Arabian Peninsula

The terrain of the Arabian Peninsula was arid and volcanic, which made it difficult for agriculture. As a result, the region was primarily a desert. Arab, nomadic, pastoral tribes roamed from place to place (oasis to oasis), following the rains and seeking pasture and water for their flocks. Nomadic survival also depended on raiding caravans and other oases. The Nomads did not consider this a crime.

There were also sedentary Arabs who settled and established communities and cities and were focused on trade and agriculture. These communities, established throughout the peninsula, consisted of various tribes. Some of the settled communities developed into small kingdoms. Pagan Arabia consisted of inhabitants commonly involved in blood feuds, women being treated as chattel, child marriage, and female infanticide.

Political Structure

In Arabia before Islam, there was a total absence of political organization in any form. With the exception of Yemen in the southwest, no part of the Arabian Peninsula had any government at any time, and the Arabs never acknowledged any authority other than that of the chiefs of their tribes. The authority of the tribal chiefs, however, rested in most cases on their character and personality. Since there was no government, there was no law and order. In the event that a crime was committed, the injured party took law into their own hands and tried to administer justice to the offender— "an eye for an eye." This system frequently led to acts of terrible cruelty. If one ever exercised any restraint, it was not because he had a question of right or wrong but because of the fear of provoking reprisals and a vendetta.

Since there were no such things as police, courts, or judges, the only protection a man could find from his enemies was within his own tribe. The tribe had an obligation to protect its members. Tribalism took precedence over right and wrong *(1).* A tribe that failed to protect its members from their enemies exposed itself to ridicule and contempt. Morality did not enter the picture.

A Warring Culture

Since Pre-Islamic Arabia did not have a government, war was a permanent fixture in Arabian society. The desert could support only a limited number of people, and the state of intertribal war maintained a rigid control over the growth of population. But the Arab peoples themselves did not see war in this light. To them, war was a pastime. Peace held no appeal, and war provided an escape from the drudgery and monotony of life in the desert. They, therefore, courted the excitement in the clash of arms.

War gave tribes in Pre-Islamic Arabia an opportunity to display their skills in archery, fencing, and horsemanship. Additionally, in war, they could distinguish themselves by their individual heroism and at the same time win glory and honor for their tribe. These nomadic tribes ranged over the peninsula and plundered the caravans and the small settlements. Many caravans and villages bought immunity from these raids by paying a fixed amount of money to the raiders.

Social Conditions

Pre-Islamic Arabia was a male-dominated society. Women had no status of any kind other than as sex objects. The number of women a man could marry was not fixed. When a man died, his son "inherited" all his wives except his own mother. Since male children were preferred over females, the custom of some Arab tribes was to bury their female infants alive. Drunkenness and gambling were common vices among the men. Relations between the sexes were extremely loose. Many women sold sex for a living, since there was little else they could do. These women flew flags on their dwellings and were called "ladies of the flags." *(2)*

Education in Arabia

Extremely few individuals in pre-Islamic Arabia could read and write. Some historians are of the opinion that the culture of the period was almost entirely oral. The greatest intellectual accomplishment of the Arabs was their poetry. They claimed that God had bestowed the most remarkable gift of the tongue upon the Arabs (its proof was their eloquence). Their greatest pride, both before and after Islam, was their eloquence and poetry. The importance of poetry to them can be gauged by the following testimony:

> *Most of the information on the economic conditions, social regime and mores of the Arabs in the fifth and sixth centuries AD, comes from ancient Arabic or pre- Islamic poetry, known for its 'photographic faithfulness' to all phases of Arabian tribal life and its environment. Specialists, therefore, accept this poetry as the 'most important and authoritative source for describing the Arab people and their customs' in this period. (3)*

The greatest compositions of the Arabs were the so-called "Golden Odes," a collection of seven poems (supposedly) of unsurpassed excellence in spontaneity, power, and eloquence. They were suspended on the *Kaaba* (sacred religious building in Mecca) as a challenge to any aspiring genius to surpass or match.

Economic Conditions

Economically, the Jews were the leaders of Pre-Islamic Arabia. They were the owners of the best cultivable lands in the northern peninsula, and they were the best farmers. They were also the entrepreneurs of such industries as existed in Arabia in those days.

Slavery was an economic institution of the Arabs. Male and female slaves were sold and bought and constituted the most oppressed class of the Arabian society. But the most powerful class of the Arabs consisted of the money-lenders. The rates of interest they charged on loans were exorbitant and were specially designed to make them richer and the borrowers poorer.

Two important urban centers of Arabia were Mecca and Medina. The citizens of Mecca were mostly merchants, traders, and money- lenders. Their caravans traveled in the summer to Syria and in the winter to Yemen. They also traveled to modern-day Bahrain in the east and modern-day Iraq in the northeast. The caravan trade was fundamental to the economy of Mecca, along with the religious pilgrimages. The caravan vocation called for considerable skill, experience, and ability.

Mecca

Mecca became an important oasis center along the "Incense Route" and an important financial center for many surrounding tribes. The main attraction was the Kaaba, the cube-shaped building whose wall housed the "Black Stone." The shrine area also contained the Sacred Well of

Zamzam *(4)*. Pilgrims throughout the Arabian Peninsula came to show their homage by circumambulating the Kaaba as part of their pilgrimage.

The Kaaba

The Kaaba (Arabic: *"cube"*) is a structure made of granite. It is approximately forty-three feet high with sides measuring thirty-six feet by forty-two feet. Inside the Kaaba, the floor is made of marble and limestone. The interior walls are clad with tiled white marble halfway to the roof, with darker trimmings along the floor. The floor of the interior stands about seven feet above the ground area. On one corner of this building is a stone known as the Black Stone. Its history is shrouded in mystery, and there is much speculation over what the stone might be. Many Muslims believe the stone is, in fact, a meteorite possessing supernatural powers and was once part of the stones in heaven. Johann L. Buchhart, in his book *Travels in Arabia* (1829), describes the Black Stone.

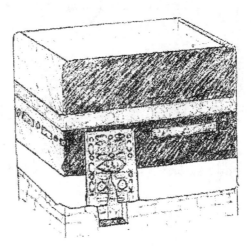

THE KAABA (Arabic for "cube", the shape of the building) It is located in the center of the Great Mosque in Mecca. (The Koran states that the Kaaba was the first House of Worship.)

Prior to the time of Muhammad, the area around the Kaaba was surrounded by 360 idols. Pilgrims from all over the Arabian Peninsula traveled to Mecca to pay homage to their particular god, gods, or goddesses.

The <u>Muslim tradition</u> states that the Kaaba was first built in Heaven. Then Adam was ordered by Allah to erect the House of God (Kaaba) on earth, but it was destroyed by the Flood. As mentioned in the previous chapter, Abraham came to the Valley of Bakkah and received a revelation from Allah to rebuild the shrine. Abraham and Ishmael constructed a stone structure. The angel Gabriel gave Ishmael a white cornerstone, which turned black from the sins of those who touched it. The stone is, therefore, sacred because it was sent from Heaven.

The Kaaba was to be the gathering place for all who wished to strengthen their faith. As the Valley of Bakkah settled because of the abundance of the spring water, the community that developed was called Bakkah and later became **Mecca**. The shrine also began drawing pilgrims and caravans. Ishmael and his mother Hagar were buried near the Kaaba.

Religion in Pre-Islamic Arabia

The Arabs were devotees of a variety of belief systems that can be classified into the following categories:

1. Idol-worshippers or polytheists. Most inhabitants of Pre-Islamic Arabia worshiped numerous idols, and each tribe had its own idol or idols and fetishes. They had turned the Kaaba in Mecca into a heathen pantheon housing 360 idols of stone and wood, which had previously been rebuilt by Abraham and dedicated to the service of One God.

2. Atheists. This group was composed of the materialists who did not believe in any god.

3. Zindiqs. They were influenced by the Persian doctrine of dualism in nature. They believed that there were two gods representing the twin forces of good and evil or light and darkness, and both were locked up in an unending struggle for supremacy.

4. Sabines. They worshiped the stars.

5. Jews. When the Romans destroyed Jerusalem in AD 70 and drove the Jews out of Palestine and Syria, many of them found new homes in Arabia. Under their influence, many Arabs also became converts to Judaism.

6. Christians. The north Arabian tribe of Ghassanid converted to Christianity. In the south, there were many Christians in Yemen, where Christianity is thought to have been originally introduced by Ethiopian invaders.

7. Monotheists. According to some scholars, there were also native pre-Islamic Arab communities who embraced the concept of Monotheism. Two cities in eastern Arabia are mentioned in the Bible: Dumah (considered to have been established by Ishmael's sixth son) and Tema (considered to have been established by Ishmael's ninth son).

The dominant belief system, however, was polytheism. At the time of Muhammad, there were 360 idols of gods and goddesses worshiped at the Kaaba in Mecca. The Kaaba was believed to be dedicated to **Hubal** and was worshiped as the greatest of the 360 idols. Hubal's likeness was described as shaped like a human and made of red agate with his right hand broken off and replaced with a golden hand *(5)*.

A story is recorded in which Muhammad's grandfather vowed to sacrifice one of his ten children. Seven arrows were placed before Hubal for divination as to which child it would be. The arrows pointed to Muhammad's father. Muhammad's father was saved, however, when ten camels were sacrificed in his place (another source claims the number of camels to be one hundred). One of the writings also claimed that Muhammad's grandfather brought the infant Muhammad before the image of Hubal.

Some scholars claim that "Allah" was one of the gods of the Meccan religion for which the shrine was dedicated. There are also scholars who claim Allah was possibly the creator god or the supreme deity of all the gods. The name "Allah" appears as supreme deity in Arabic stone inscriptions <u>centuries before</u> Islam. Muhammad's father's name was Abd-Allah, meaning *"servant of Allah."*

The Quraysh Tribe, during the time of Muhammad, were the protectors of the Kaaba. (We will explore in Chapter 3 how and why Muhammad came in conflict with his own tribe in regards to the Kaaba.)

(1)   **Asabiyya: "Group or Tribal unity; social solidarity"**
(2)   **Dhat-er-rayyat: "Ladies of the flags"**
(3)   **E. A. Belyaev, Arabs, Islam and the Arab Caliphate in the Early Middle Ages, 1969**
(4)   **Genesis 21:14–19**
(5)   **Hisham Ibn Al-Kalbi, Book of Idols**

THE CRESENT MOON AND STAR

The crescent moon and star symbol actually pre-dates Islam by several thousand years. Information on the origins of the symbol is difficult to confirm, but most sources agree that these ancient celestial symbols were in use by the peoples of Central Asia and Siberia in their worship of sun, moon, and sky gods. There are also reports that the crescent moon and star were used to represent the Carthaginian goddess Tanit or the Greek goddess Diana.

The city of Byzantium (later known as Constantinople and Istanbul) adopted the crescent moon as its symbol. According to some reports, they chose it in honor of the goddess Diana. Others indicate that it dates back to a battle in which the Romans defeated the Goths on the first day of a lunar month. In any event, the crescent moon was featured on the city's flag even before the birth of Christ.

Early Muslim Community

The early Muslim community did not really have a symbol. During the time of the Muhammad, Islamic armies and caravans flew simple solid-colored flags (generally black, green, or white) for identification purposes. In later generations, the Muslim leaders continued to use a simple black, white, or green flag with no markings, writing, or symbolism on it.

Ottoman Empire

It wasn't until the Ottoman Empire that the crescent moon and star became affiliated with the Muslim world. When the Turks conquered Constantinople (Istanbul) in 1453, they adopted the city's existing flag and symbol. Legend holds that the founder of the Ottoman Empire, Osman, had a dream in which the crescent moon stretched from one end of the earth to the other. Taking this as a good omen, he chose to keep the crescent and make it the symbol of his dynasty. There is speculation that the five points on the star represent the five pillars of Islam, but this is pure conjecture. The five points were not standard on the Ottoman flags, and are still not standard on flags used in the Muslim world today.

CHAPTER 3

MUHAMMAD

(The Prophet/Apostle/Messenger)

As we begin our search for the "real" Muhammad, we find that there were many names ascribed to Muhammad as well as many myths in order to elevate the religion of Islam. It should also be noted that Muhammad was <u>not</u> an uncommon given name in Arabian communities prior to the birth of the prophet. Also, I have chosen certain stories regarding the prophet from the many that were written long after his death by Muslim scholars to enhance the importance of the Koran and their prophet. I should first mention three other Muslim sacred writings where many of the stories and reports of the prophet are recorded several years after his death.

> **Hadith**: "narrative or report." Islamic beliefs, values, and practices, also telling the story of the origin of the religion and the actions and traditions of the prophet.
>
> **Sunnah**: "usual practice." The "practice" of the prophet; what he did as an example for his followers.
>
> **Sira**: Stories of the prophet intended as historical accounts for his veneration and elevation to near-deity level.

Muhammad created: a new religion by incorporating elements of the existing religions of the Arabia Peninsula; new methods of war; and a political system that included a strict legal code. Some people have branded him as the world's greatest warrior. No one today wages war in the name of a military leader, but thousands and thousands of people—Muslims and non-Muslims alike—are dying today in wars instigated in the name of Muhammad.

To have some understanding of Islam, we must have some knowledge of the life of Muhammad and his teachings—or an interpretation of his teachings.

His Family and Early Years

One Islamic source states that Muhammad's father was a member of the Bani Hashim Clan, which was part of the Quraysh Tribe. Both his father and mother were members of the Quraysh Tribe, who were the keepers (protectors) of the **Kaaba**, the holy shrine in Mecca. Shortly after his mother and father were married, his father went on a caravan trading trip. Arriving at his destination, he became sick and died. His wife was pregnant, and after the death of her husband, she had her child in 570 AD in Mecca. What was the baby's name.. ? Was it Muhammad ibn Abdallah? Probably not!

Muhammad's mother had a dream in which her husband informed her that she would have a son, and she should name him **Ahmad** ("to praise"). Another Islamic source suggested his birth name was **Pbuh**. Other sources suggest that his birth name was **Kunya**. I shall refer to him as **Kunya** until a certain event allegedly happened to him at the Kaaba.

When Kunya was six years old, his mother died. For a period of about two years, he was under the care of his grandfather. Kunya was ten years old when his grandfather died, and he was sent to his uncle. One of the stories tells of his uncle taking him on a trading trip to Damascus, Syria. There, a Christian monk said he saw in Kunya the markings of a true prophet. Kunya continued to travel on business trips with and later for his uncle throughout the region, including to Jerusalem. He became a successful businessman as a caravan agent and produce merchant, and his trips brought him into contact with Christians and Jews alike. Khadajah, a forty-year-old widow who was a wealthy businesswoman in Mecca, hired Kunya to work for her. When Kunya was twenty-five, he married her, and she allegedly had seven children to Kunya, with only one surviving infancy: a daughter, **Fatima**.

Kunya Receives a New Name

The story is told of how Kunya became **Muhammad**. The sacred building of the Kaaba in Mecca contained the Black Stone, which is purported to have come down from Heaven. A flood dislodged the Black Stone, and when the water subsided, there was much debate as to who would have the honor of replacing the "Holy Stone". It was decided that the first man to enter the court at a certain time would have the honor of replacing the Black Stone. Kunya entered the court and was given the honor of replacing the Stone. He took off his cloak and placed the Stone on it. He then gathered the rival tribal chiefs and told them to lift the Stone on the garment to the level of its proper location. As they did, he slid the Stone into place amid loud praises. Kunya became **"the praised one,"** in Arabic. . . . *Muhammad*!

Muhammad's "Religious Experience"

According to Islamic tradition, Muhammad retired to the wilderness for religious purposes when he was forty years old (AD 610) *(1)*. In a cave on the slopes of Mount Hira, he thought about religion. He decided that the primitive religion of his own people needed to be improved and made more like Christianity and Judaism.

Strange things began to happen in that cave. He heard bells ringing and vague voices. He went into a trance-like fit or seizure. And then the angel Gabriel appeared, giving him a message from Allah. He returned home to his wife and related his experience to her and his nephew, Ali.

His wife was convinced it was a Divine revelation. One Islamic source claimed that she recorded this message from Allah, since Muhammad was illiterate *(2)*. Her uncle, a Christian priest, was (*supposed*) to have confirmed Muhammad's prophetic status.

There were other revelations Muhammad received from God, whom he called **Allah**. He was commanded to pray and to warn his fellow men to change their conduct. Following the experience he had in his contact with Christians and Jews, he proclaimed: There is only <u>one</u> God, Allah, the creating and judging God. He warned of the last judgment and condemned moral depravity, and he claimed that all the idols (360) in the Kaaba were false.

As Muhammad began preaching and teaching about his new revelation, he had some converts, mostly from poorer clans, and a significant number of women. His message emphasized that one must "surrender" to the laws of God (the word *Islam* means "to surrender"). His converts called themselves *Muslims*: "those who submits to Allah."

Muhammad retained the following customs from the "pagan" Arabs: polygamy, slavery, easy divorce, circumcision, ceremonial cleanliness, covering the head to prevent evil spirits from entering the body, and many gestures such as raised hands and prostrating on ground.

> *Muhammad was not an original thinker: he did not formulate any new ethical principles, but merely borrowed from the prevailing cultural milieu.*
>
> *—Ibn Warraq*

The Meccans feared their pilgrimage industry would be threatened with his preaching and his teachings, and they became hostile toward Muhammad and his followers. After the death of his wife and his uncle, who had been his protector, the persecution against Muhammad became even more severe. In the year 622 AD, he and his small group of about 80 followers escaped from Mecca and traveled 210 miles north to **Medina**. This event of traveling to Medina, (***Hijrah:*** "emigration") was later viewed with such importance that Muslims declared 622 AD as **day one** of the Islamic calendar.

Medina

Medina was a city of beauty situated in one of the most fertile areas of Arabia. Various tribes, including Jewish and Christian tribes, lived in and around Medina. Jews played an important part of the social and commercial life of Medina. Muhammad's grandmother was a member of one of the tribes in Medina.

Muhammad's first action in Medina was to build a **mosque (3)**. A band of tribal warriors accepted Muhammad as a prophet and became Muslims. Muhammad reached two agreements between him and the clans of Medina. The agreements established that the Muslims who followed Muhammad from Mecca would become equal to the eight clans of Medina. The new converts of Medina were called **Ansar**, or "*helpers.*" Collectively, the nine tribes formed the first Muslim community. The agreements also regulated the relations between the Muslims and the Jewish tribes in Medina. (Some of the Jews believed he was the messiah.)

As we have mentioned before, Muhammad was illiterate, but he learned a great deal from interfacing with the Jewish tribes, their customs, stories, and practices. There were also Christian tribes with whom he also had contact, learning about Jesus' life and teachings.

> *The Arab Prophet's message was an eclectic composite of religious ideas and regulations. The ideas were suggested to him by contacts, which stirred him deeply, with Jewish, Christian, and other elements.*
>
> *—Ignaz Goldziher*

Muhammad later became convinced that the Jews falsified their scriptures to conceal the foretelling of his mission as the prophet of Allah when they questioned his role.

Muhammad and his followers began raiding caravans, with Muhammad often leading the raids. He was no longer a purely religious, peaceful, warning prophet as he had been in Mecca. Muhammad became Allah's war-waging monarch in Medina, implementing threats and coercion. In Medina, Muhammad became a warlord.

In order to incorporate the Jewish tribe into Islam, he suggested offering to pray facing Jerusalem. The Jewish tribe rejected his prophetic call. He then led his warriors in killing all the Jewish men, taking their women and children as slaves, and dividing the booty among his warriors. He also engaged in warfare against the Christian tribes. Muhammad was on a mission of combining religion and politics with "Holy" war, later referred to as "**Jihad**" *(4)*.

Muhammad did not teach peace and tolerance but led armies and ordered assassinations of his enemies. He did allow negotiated settlements but only in the service of the ultimate goal of Islamic conquest. He became a prophet of war, a raider, assessing revenge, assassinations, and deceit. He commanded his followers to kill and butcher those who opposed Islam. It is said that two-thirds of the biographies of Muhammad concern battles he undertook— as many as seventy military engagements. He led several small skirmishes against Meccans in AD 623 and 624.

The Spoils of Victory

One of the spoils of victory was not only the animals and valuables but slaves. Ibn Qayyim al-Jawziyya, scholar and Islamic historian, states in his book *Zad al-Ma'ad,* part 1, page 160:

> *Muhammad had many male and female slaves. He used to buy and sell them, but he purchased more*

slaves than he sold. He once sold one black slave for two. His purchases of slaves were more than he sold.

Muhammad had a number of black slaves. One of them was named "Mahran." Muhammad forced him to do more labor than the average man. Whenever Muhammad went on a trip and he, or his people, got tired of carrying their stuff, he made Mahran carry it. Mahran said, "Even if I were already carrying the load of six or seven donkeys while we were on a journey, anyone who felt weak would throw his clothes or his shield or his sword on me so I would carry that, a heavy load." Tabari and Jawziyya both record this, so Islam accepts this as true.

There are hundreds of hadiths that deal with slavery. Whole chapters of hadith are dedicated to dealing with the taxation, treatment, sale, and jurisprudence of slaves. In addition to this, numerous hadiths mention slaves and their relation to their Muslim masters. Muslims took female slaves and had sex with them. Muhammad approved of this. He only admonished them not to practice coitus interruptus.

The Koran also instructs Muslims *not* to force their female slaves into prostitution (24:34) and even allows Muslims to marry slaves if they so desire (4:24) and to free them at times as a penalty for crime or sin (4:92, 5:89, 58:3). The law even allows slaves to buy their liberty if they meet certain conditions set forth by their masters (24:33).

Flight to Jerusalem (The Night Journey): *The Night Journey* (5) took place ten years after Muhammad became a prophet. Muhammad had been in his home city of Mecca, at his cousin's home. He then went to the Great Mosque. While he was resting at the Kaaba, the angel Gabriel appeared to him followed by a White Stallion (6). Muhammad mounted the White Stallion and, in the company of Gabriel, traveled to the "farthest mosque." The location of this mosque is not explicitly stated but is generally accepted to mean the Temple Mount in Jerusalem. A mosque was built on the site called "The Dome of the Rock." It is built over and around the ancient sacrificial stone where Muhammad descended, riding the White Stallion from Heaven.

He dismounted from the Stallion, prayed, and re-mounted the Stallion, who took him to the various heavens to meet the earlier prophets and then Allah. Allah instructed Muhammad to tell his followers that they were to offer prayers five times a day. At the urging of Moses, Muhammad returned to Allah. The Stallion then transported Muhammad back to Mecca.

This Night Journey to Jerusalem is why the Dome of the Rock is the third most important Islamic mosque and Jerusalem the third most important city to Muslims.

The Koran refers to Muhammad's mystic travel to the Heavens:

> **Glory to (Allah) Who did take His servant for a Journey by night from the Sacred Mosque to the farthest Mosque, whose precincts We did bless, in order that We might show him some of Our Signs: for He is the One Who heareth and seeth (all things).**
>
> **—Koran 17:1**

The Battle of the Oasis of Badr

Muhammad had always set his sights on returning to Mecca and purging the Kaaba of the false idol gods. In order to secure food and provisions for his followers, Muhammad decided to attack a caravan returning from Mecca. The caravan leader discovered the plot and received reinforcements from Mecca. When Muhammad and his warriors arrived at the Oasis of Badr, they encountered an army of 1,000 Meccans. However, Muhammad's army of 300 warriors defeated the Meccans who, unlike Muhammad's warriors, were not skilled fighters.

The battle took place on March 13, AD 624. To Muhammad's followers, this victory reinforced and offered convincing proof that he was a true prophet of Allah.

Muhammad then began conquering Arab populations and territories throughout the desert area. To his "enemies," he offered conversion, death, or servitude. The enemies' surrender treaty allowed the conquered to continue to cultivate the land, but they had to pay a heavy tax. They did not have any political rights, and Muhammad had the right to cancel the treaty and expel them whenever he desired, which he often did. The conquered non-Muslim people were considered *"Protected People"(7).*

But there were also defeats. Muhammad told his followers that their defeats were punishment for not fighting wholeheartedly for Allah.

The Return to Mecca

Muhammad set his sights on returning to Mecca and purging the Kaaba of the false idol gods. In AD 630, he led a 10,000-member army back to Mecca. He encountered little resistance from his tribe, who were the protectors of the Kaaba. Mecca surrendered, and all the idols were destroyed. The Kaaba was cleansed. Thus, the leading Meccan officials embraced Islam with little bloodshed.

This was not, however, the end of warfare for Muhammad. During this same year, the pagan tribes wanted to regain the Kaaba and formed a coalition to do so. Muhammad led an army of 12,000 against them at Hunayn in a deep ravine. The forces of Muhammad were victorious, and the booty from the victory was enormous because the pagan tribes had brought everything they had with them: 6,000 women and 24,000 camels.

Although Mecca was now under Muslim authority, the pagan Arabs, who had not broken their treaties nor supported anyone who *had* broken their treaties, were still permitted to perform their pilgrimage until their treaty expired. When their treaty expired, they would be treated like the other "idolaters" and not permitted to perform their religious pilgrimage to Mecca.

> *Interpreter of the will of Allah, Muhammad combined the political power of a military leader, the religious power and the functions of a judge.*

—*Bat Ye'or*

The Death of Muhammad

Muhammad returned to Medina to his "***Ummah***," the community of Islamic people. Shortly thereafter, he supposedly departed Medina with 90,000 Muslims from every part of Arabia to perform the pilgrimage of the **Hajj** *(8).* This is often referred to as his "farewell pilgrimage." When he returned to Medina, he had a painful illness, and those who saw him at the mosque thought they saw signs of death in his face.

Early Islamic scholars and writers provide us with some interesting circumstances surrounding his death recorded in the **hadith** (the words, actions, and habits of Muhammad). Following the conquest of the Jewish town of Khaibar, which contained several Jewish tribes, Muhammad took Safiyah as a wife and then ordered the torture and beheading of her husband Kinana, the chief of the Jews at Khaibar.

> *A Jewess brought a poisoned (cooked) sheep for the Prophet who ate from it. She was brought to the Prophet and he was askee said, "No." I continued to see the effect of the poison on the palate of the mouth of Allah's Apostle. (9)*

Muhammad asked her,

What induced you to do what you have done?

She replied,

> *You have done to my people what You have done. You
> have killed my father, my uncle and my husband, so I
> said to myself, "If you are a prophet, the foreleg will
> inform you;" and others have said, "If you are a king
> we will get rid of you." (10)*

From one of the six major hadith collections, we read,

> *The Prophet in his ailment in which he died, used to
> say, "O 'Aisha! I still feel the pain caused by the food I
> ate at Khaibar, and at this time, I feel as if <u>my aorta</u>
> is being cut from that poison." (11)*

What makes this comment interesting is that the Koran 69:44–46 states:

> *And if he (Muhammad) had fabricated against Us
> some of the sayings (Revelations), we would certainly
> have seized him by the right hand, then We would
> certainly have cut off his aorta.*

From his own statement, we must conclude that God had taken his life
because of false revelations, which, therefore, makes him a **<u>false</u>** prophet. *(12)*

We are told that even on his deathbed, Muhammad issued orders and cursed Christians and Jews.

> *Then he (Muhammad) ordered them to do three things. He said, "Turn the pagans out of the Arabian Peninsula; respect and give gifts to the foreign delegations as you have seen me dealing with them."*

Said bin Jubar. The sub-narrator said that Ibn Abbas kept quiet as regards to the third order, or said, "I forgot it." *(13)*

> *On his deathbed Allah's Apostle put a sheet over his face and when he felt hot, he would remove it from his face. When is that state (of putting and removing the sheet) he said, "May Allah's Curse be on the Jews and the Christians for they will build places of worship at the graves of the prophets." (By that) he intended to warn (the Muslim) from that they (i.e. Jews and Christians) had done. (14)*

He died in his dwelling with his wife **Aisha** at his side on June 8, AD 632.

> *Aisha added: "He died on the day of my usual turn at my house. Allah took him unto Him while His head was between my chest and my neck and his saliva was mixed with my saliva." (15)*

Muhammad's Death Erection

According to Abu al-Fida (AD 1273–1331), a Muslim geographer and historian, Muhammad suffered from a death erection. His son-in- law and cousin, Ali, washed his body after his death and exclaimed, *"O prophet, thy penis is erect unto the sky!"*

Mohammed was buried in his own house, which had already served as a mosque for some years. The mosque still exists and is counted as the second most important mosque in Islam, and Medina, the second most holy city. He did not designate a successor. Islam claims that Muhammad was the last and final Messenger (prophet) of Allah. He is called "*The Perfect man*," and *"Whosoever obeys the Messenger, thereby obeys God!" (16)*

Muhammad's Wives

Authors, scholars, and historians offer varying opinions on the number of Muhammad's wives, ranging from nine to nineteen. One Islamic source lists the following:

- 19 wives
- 14 broken engagements
- 10 refused proposals

Another Islamic source states that he was married to thirteen women, including eleven at one time. He relegated them to either consecutive days or all in one night. In addition, he also had several slave girls and concubines with whom he supposedly had sex, sometimes on the same days on which they watched their husbands and/or fathers die at the hands of his army. It appears odd that the founder or creator of the world's most sexually restrictive religion was one of the most sexually indulgent characters in history.

In two of Islam's most sacred writings (*Sunnah* and *Hadith*), Muhammad consummated his marriage to **Aisha** when she was only nine years of age *(17)*. Aisha took her dolls with her to his house so that she had something to play with when the prophet was not having sex with her *(18)*. Muhammad's wives had to be available for the prophet's fondling even when they were having their menstrual period *(19)*. *"The Prophet used to go round* (to have sexual relations) *all his wives in one night, and he had nine wives."(20)*

31

Islamic Historians' Perspective on Muhammad's Genealogy

Islamic historians believe that Muhammad's ancestry can be traced back to Ishmael. As proof of this, they refer to the genealogy written around AD 770–775 by Ibn Ishak. However, according to Dr. Rafat Amari, historians claim that the family of Muhammad lived in Yemen and that one of his ancestors put together an alliance of several families to form the Qu rajah Tribe, who were Muhammad's descendants. This Tribe did not migrate to Mecca until the 5th century. Thus, Dr. Amari concludes that Muhammad's family was not connected to any Ishmaelite tribe because his tribe could not have lived in the same location as any of the Ishmaelite tribes any time throughout history.

Muhammad and the Koran

The orthodox Islamic teaching is that the Koran, as it has reached us today, is the perfect, timeless, and unchanging words of Allah in the Arabic language. However, the <u>authentic</u> Koran exists only in Heaven.

Although the Islamic historians claim that the Koran was either written or recorded by Muhammad and/or his wife and his scribes during his lifetime, nothing could be further from the truth. Muhammad was illiterate. He commanded his followers to memorize his revelations. Therefore, the segments of the Koran were passed down <u>orally</u> until after his death.

> *When Muhammad died, there existed no singular codex of the sacred text. While the memorizers were numerous, no one of them knew the whole. The revelations were scattered and were threatened with being lost. (21)*

Chapter 5 is devoted to pursuing this further with a brief overview of the content of the Koran.

(1) The content of this first revelation is supposedly recorded in the Koran.
(2) One tradition has Muhammad being served by forty-five scribes after his wife's death.
(3) Masjid: a place of prostration
(4) Can be an inner spiritual struggle or the struggle against enemies of Islam.
(5) The Lailat al Miraj: Hadiths supply other details about the Night Journey.
(6) Al-Buraq ("lightning") is a steed in Islamic mythology; a creature from the heavens that transported the prophets. Most notably, Buraq carried the Islamic prophet Muhammad from Mecca to Jerusalem and back during the "Night Journey," as recounted in hadith literature. Vuckovic, Brooke Olson, *Heavenly Journeys, Earthly Concerns,* (New York: Routledge, 2004)
(7) Dhimma: "protected person"
(8) Religious pilgrimage
(9) Hadith: Narrated by Anas bi Malik
(10) Sunni scholar and biographer (AD 784–845) ibn Sa'd, page 252
(11) Hadith: Narrated by 'Aisha-Sahih Bukhari 5:59:713
(12) For further information on this conclusion, David Wood can be viewed on YouTube, or visit his websites at: www.answeringMuslims.com and www. answeringIslam.com.
(13) Hadith: Sahih Bukhari 5:59:716
(14) Hadith: Sahih Bukhari 4:56:660
(15) Hadith: Narrated by Aisha-Sahih Bukhari 7:62:144
(16) Koran 4:80
(17) Hadith 8:3311
(18) Hadith 73:151
(19) Hadith 6:300
(20) Hadith 62:6
(21) Islam by Caesar E. Farah, page 95

The hand symbol is called the Hand of Fatima by Muslims, named for the daughter of Muhammed, and is sometimes said to symbolize the five pillars or tenets of Islam.

This Maze-like ornamental square of angular kufic script is made up of the names of the ten most revered companions of Muhammad.

CHAPTER 4

THE EXPANSION OF ISLAM

The Successor(s)

Muhammad did not prepare anyone to succeed him as the leader of the Muslim Community. However, immediately after his death in AD 632, Muhammad's father-in-law **Abu Bakr** succeeded him as leader of the Muslim Community. Abu was the father of **Aisha**, Muhammad's favorite wife and his child bride. He continued the effort to abolish paganism among the Arab tribes and to incorporate Arabia into a region controlled by the political power of Medina.

Abu's reign lasted a little over two years. He was succeeded by Umar ibn al-Khattab. It was probably under his reign that the term *"Caliph"* *(1)* came to be used as the title for the civil, religious, and military head of the Islamic State or *"Caliphate"* and the successor of Muhammad. Abu and his three immediate successors are known as the *"perfect"* or *"rightly guided"* Caliphs. They were basically elected or chosen by the elders of the various tribes *(2)*.

Muslims organized themselves according to the rule of the Caliphate for centuries after the death of the Prophet Mohammed. In life, Mohammed taught that Muslims must believe that he received direct messages from God and that he serves as both religious leader and temporal ruler of the legions drawn to his teachings. But when the Prophet died, leaving no heir, the search was on for a successor— which is what *caliph* means. The Caliphate (or *succession*) is the area or lands that he rules, and he commands the governing body that claims dominion over all believers.

The Islamic State (Caliphate) expanded very rapidly under these four Caliphs through successes both in converting unbelievers to Islam and by military conquests of the Muslim Community's opponents. These wars that expanded the Muslim religion were accomplished through the devotion of the faithful to the concept of "**Jihad**" *(3)*. This expansion is understandable; the example had been successfully accomplished by Muhammad, who had established this new religion through the conversions and conquests of those who stood against him.

Also aiding in the expansion of Islam were the political upheavals occurring outside Arabia. There had been long wars between the Byzantine and Persian empires, and there were devastating problems in Syria and Egypt.

In AD 626, Muslim armies conquered Syria and then subdued Iraq, Persia, and, by AD 640, the greater part of Egypt. By the end of the reigns of the first four successors to Muhammad (caliphs), Islam had increased its territory to most of the Near East and Africa.

With its new conquests, Islam was apparently governed well. Non-believers either embraced the new religion, were put to death, or paid a tax *(4)*. Of course, the threat of death and additional taxing led to many converts to the new religion. One of the positive factors of this new religion was that it embraced people of all colors and cultures, even though, at times, it initially became a factor in creating tension between the Arab people and the non-Arab people.

The expansion of Islam was astounding. **In just one hundred years** after Muhammad first claimed prophethood, Islam conquered all of Arabia and then expanded and conquered as far west as Spain and as far east as Afghanistan. The Islamic State became the largest empire the world had yet known, controlling some of the most important centers of civilization. Of the five great urban centers of Christianity in the sixth and seventh centuries AD, three of them now fell under Islamic rule (Jerusalem, Alexandria, and Antioch), with only Rome and Constantinople still under Christian rule.

From this point on, much of Mediterranean history would be characterized by the struggles between the Christian and Islamic faiths, the Christians holding the north side of the Mediterranean and the Muslims the south side. The battlegrounds were in Spain, Jerusalem, and Constantinople.

The Beginning of Divisions

The first three successors to Muhammad were chosen in consultation with the elders and leaders of the Muslim Community and were members of the Quraysh tribe in Mecca (Muhammad's tribe). The fourth successor (caliph) was **Ali ibn Abi Talib**, who was the prophet's cousin and son-in-law (he was married to Fatima, Muhammad's daughter to his first wife). Ali took part in the early caravan raids from Mecca and most of the battles fought by the Muslim Community. He was appointed caliph by Muhammad's Companions (his elders and close friends) in AD 656 after the third caliph was assassinated.

Ali convinced the elders and leaders of the Muslim Community that the successorship of the Caliphship should remain in the family of the prophet. His decision was not popular. His followers were later called "**Shiites**" *(5)*. Ali's reign saw civil unrest, and, in 661, he was attacked and assassinated. Most biographical sources agree that he was a pious Muslim, devoted to Islam, and a just ruler.

A great dispute arose over the legitimate successorship to the caliphship. "**Sunni**" *(6)* Muslims rejected the Shiite teaching that Ali was the true successor of Muhammad. These two major Islamic "denominations" fought battles and wars against one another. At other times, they cooperated and lived peacefully with one another.

The Spread of Islam Continues: In AD 661, a relative of the third Caliph proclaimed himself Caliphate and made Damascus his capital. He established the Umayyad Dynasty, which lasted until AD 750.

The Umayyad military campaigns of conquest were mainly successful. Their naval battles conquered Cyprus, Rhodes, and a number of Aegean islands that served as bases for attacks on Constantinople. Their westward campaigns across North Africa were much more successful. The next step in their efforts was to cross the Strait of Gibraltar, into the weak kingdom of the Visigoths in Spain. By 718, the kingdom of the Visigoths was conquered.

The Muslims advanced across the Pyrenees and gained a foothold in southwest France. However, they were defeated that same year by the Byzantine emperor. Then, in 732, they were defeated in the Battle of Tours, France by Charles Martel. This defeat halted their northward expansion into Europe. Meanwhile, the Muslims had been expanding eastward into Central Asia. By the ninth century, they could claim lands as distant as Turkestan and the Indus Valley.

The new conquests of Islam were governed with well-documented efficiency and flexibility. The centralization of authority aided in the incorporation of new peoples, and unbelievers in the conquered territories became increasingly interested in the new religion and accepted Islam. The imposition of a tax on all non-Muslims obviously encouraged many to become converts. However, there were non- Muslims who participated in government activities, served as minor officials, and prospered financially.

Comparing the Rise of Islam to the Rise of Christianity

Both faiths began as the teachings of a single man; both witnessed extremely rapid, almost miraculous growth in just a few centuries. However, the method by which the two faiths spread could not have been more different.

For the first four centuries AD, **Christianity** spread by peaceful conversion. Then, once it became adopted as the official religion of the Roman Empire in AD 380, Christians had sufficient power to dominate, intimidate, and even suppress other religions. The followers of **Islam**, on the other hand, used military force from the very beginning of their history, particularly during the life of Muhammad. Towns were brought under Islamic rule by conquest, and Christian churches and temples were usually converted into mosques.

Christians and Jews were treated a little fairer than followers of other religions, as they were considered similar and would be tolerated as long as they paid the **Jizyah**, the special tax that Jews and Christians had to pay the Islamic state in order to practice their religion, albeit with many restrictions. In the first few centuries of Islamic rule, there is little evidence of forced conversion of Christians and Jews; nevertheless, there were considerable economic and social pressures to convert to the ruling religion.

(1) Caliph (Arabic: khalifah) means "successor"; a person considered a religious successor to Muhammad and a leader **of the entire Muslim community.**

(2) **Shura means "consultation" (loosely considered to be an earlier form of Islamic democracy.)**

(3) **Jihad: the Arabic word meaning "striving, applying oneself, struggling, persevering"**

(4) **Jizyah: the per capita tax levied on non-Muslim subjects. (see Appendix)**

(5) **Shiat-u-Ali: "The party of Ali," or "followers of Ali"**

(6) Sunni: "Usual practice; customs; traditions;" practical applications of the Sunnah.

CHAPTER 5

KORAN (QUR'AN) AND OTHER SACRED WRITINGS

Traditional and orthodox Muslims believe that the Koran was completed during the lifetime of Muhammad. Modern scholarship has debunked this assertion, much to the resistance of Muslims. When did the Koran evolve, and who wrote and/or copied it? I will let the scholars speak to this. We will look at its content, stories, teachings, and claims.

The Arabic word for Koran, **Qur'an**, means *"the recitation."* According to orthodox Muslim scholars and historians, Arabic was to be the sole language of the Koran because it is the copy of the archetype and perfect copy of the one in Heaven. It was also the language the archangel Gabriel spoke during his revelations to Muhammad and the language in which they were to be preserved.

The Koran is Allah's final message to mankind. Even today, the adherents are taught to recite the Koran in Arabic, regardless of their native language. Since Arabic is such a difficult language, with variations of scripts, changing characters, and variable pronunciation, the recitation of the Koran differs from one school to another. *"Recitation of the Qur'an, even today . . . differs from one school to another of those concerned with the study of the Qur'an."* ***(1)***

The revelations given to Muhammad by Gabriel were to be memorized and recited. No single manuscript (codex) existed when Muhammad died. *"While memorizers were numerous, no one of them knew the whole."* *(2)* It is the opinion of some modern non-Islamic historians that *"as we have it, it is not the work of Muhammad . . . but a precipitate of the social and cultural pressures of the first two Islamic centuries."(3)*

It appears to be evident that the Koran, as it was compiled, underwent transformation during the one hundred years or so following the prophet's death. Modern religious scholars (non-Muslim), believe that the Koran was canonized (fixed or standardized) somewhere between 250 and 300 years after the death of Muhammad.

Structure and Content

The Koran is divided into 114 chapters (*Surah*) and 6,200 to 6,240 verses (*ayah*) and is comprised of 80,000 words. According to Crone and Cook, the Koran is *"Strikingly lacking in overall structure; frequently obscure and inconsequential in both language and content . . . and given to repetition of whole passages in variant versions."(4)*

The Koran's **main messages** are:

- One God
- Reward for good actions/punishment for evil actions
- Day of Judgment
- Heaven (Paradise) and Hell
- The Resurrection
- Angels who communicate between God and Man
- Recognition of certain prophets
  o 18 Old Testament
  o 3 New Testament (including Jesus)
- **Most important people**:
  o Adam o Noah
  o Abraham

- o Moses
- o Jesus
- o Muhammad

Islam recognizes the validity of the Old Testament—especially the Psalms and the Torah—and also the validity of the Gospels of the New Testament. It accepts previous revelations of Biblical prophets as valid. However, Muslim scholars and historians believe that the doctrines, practices, and mistakes of the various writers had to be corrected because people continually strayed from the teachings of the prophets. These wrong practices and doctrines were corrected more "perfectly" through the revelations to Muhammad.

It is obvious that the content of the Koran is dependent on the Jewish and Christian scriptures. Robert Spencer, in his book *The Truth About Muhammad*, also believes there is a dependence upon Zoroastrianism.

Biblical stories that are retold in the Koran include:

- Story of Creation
- Adam and Eve
- Cain and Abel
- Noah and the Flood
- Lot and the destruction of the evil cities
- Joseph
- Moses and the Exodus
- David and Goliath
- Solomon and the Queen of Sheba
- Afflictions of Job
- Birth of Jesus

The Koran does not detail the stories, but they are often scattered among several different chapters. The Story of Creation in the Koran is recorded in bits and pieces. For example, in the Story of Creation, Chapter 6:96–97, day and night and the stars are created; Chapter 13:3, mountains, rivers, fruits, and day and night are created; Chapter 57:4, the Creation took **six** "periods of time"; chapter 41:9–12 indicates that the Creation took **eight** "periods of time"; and Chapter 79:27–33, the Creation Story is given again.

The Story of Moses is another example of how stories are scattered among the various chapters of the Koran. (Chapters 28:2–31; 10:88–89; 7:10–170; 44:17–59).

Jesus of the Koran

The Koran makes the following references to Jesus: *(5)*

- Jesus was born of the Virgin Mary. (19:19–21)
- Jesus was strengthened by the Holy Spirit. (2:87)
- Jesus was given revelation by Allah and made a prophet. (19:30)
- Jesus was taken bodily into Heaven. (3:55)
- Jesus was created the same as Adam, from dust. (3:59)
- Jesus was <u>not</u> crucified. (4:157)
- Jesus was a miracle worker. (2:253)
- Jesus did not say to worship him of Mary. (5:116)
- Allah sent the Gospel to Jesus. (5:46; 57:27)
- You are cursed if you say Jesus was God's son. (9:30)
- Jesus talked when he was a baby. (19:29–30)
- Jesus was not the son of Allah. (19:34–35)
- Jesus was the son of Mary. (33:7)
- Jesus was no more than God's servant (prophet; messenger). (43:57–59)
- Jesus said to fear Allah and obey him (Jesus). (43:63)

There are many other verses that mention Jesus, but they are repetitive.

Author Robert Spencer offers the following statement regarding the Koran:

> *The worst mistake that Islamic scholars and historians made was their insistence that the Qur'an was the literal word of Allah, which closed the possibility of interpretation and intellectual ideas and freedom of thought which is the only way Islamic world is going to progress into the 21ˢᵗ century. (6)*

I would add to Spencer's statement: It is also modern Muslims' insistence that the Koran can only be read and quoted in Arabic and that God only hears Arabic and communicates in Arabic. This is equivalent to the former use of only Latin in the Roman Catholic Mass, which severely limited the average worshiper's awareness of what the scriptures were actually saying.

Modern Scholarship and the Koran

In an article in *The Atlantic Monthly*, January 1999, Toby Lester has some very relevant information regarding the Koran. The article's premise asks, is the Koran the complete word of God from Heaven, or is it, rather, a historical document that has evolved through history? The article is regarding manuscript and parchment findings in recent years.

During the restoration in 1972 of the Great Mosque of Sana'a in Yemen, laborers were working on the roof of the mosque and discovered an area that contained old parchment, paper documents, damaged books, and pages of Arabic texts, fused together by centuries of weather conditions and damaged by rodents and insects. The workers put them in sacks and stashed them in one of the mosque's minarets.

At some point, the Yemen Antiquities Authority's president recognized the importance of this find. He determined that some of the pieces of parchment appeared to date back to the seventh and eighth centuries. . . . They were fragments of what might possibly be the oldest Korans in existence. Even more interesting was the fact that these fragments deviated from the "official" Koran. If these seventh and eighth-century fragments were authentic, this would be contrary to the Islamic claim that the Koran is the "perfect" word of Allah.

In 1981, these fragments were examined by Ger-d Pruin, a specialist in Arabic calligraphy and Koran paleography. He recognized the antiquity and, in contrast to the present Koran, many textual variations, along with unconventional verse order and other unusual items. He began to see that the Koran was an "evolving" text rather than the words of Allah revealed in its entirety to the Prophet Muhammad in the seventh century AD. Pruin noted that every fifth sentence lacked clarity, and the document was devoid of any overall unity.

Another professor of Islamic studies, R. Stephen Humphrey, states, *"If the Koran is a historical document, then the whole Islamic struggle of fourteen centuries is effectively meaningless."*

However, the majority of Muslims around the world are unlikely to question the orthodox understanding and interpretation of the Koran, nor accept the evolution of the Koran over the centuries. Nor does the majority have much knowledge of Islamic history.

THE OTHER SACRED WRITINGS OF ISLAM Hadith

Hadiths are the purported words, actions, and habits of Muhammad. It is second only to the Koran in matters of Islamic Law. The *hadith literature* is based on reports that were in circulation in the Muslim communities after the death of Muhammad. The *hadith reports* were not compiled by any central authority but were gathered into large collections during the eighth and ninth centuries. Each hadith consists of two parts: first, the text which describes the prophet's words and/or actions; and second, the chain of transmission by which the report was communicated. Each hadith has been classified by Muslim clerics and jurists as either "authentic," "good," or "weak." However, there is no agreement as to which hadith falls into each category *(7).*

Sunnah

The **Sunnah** is the record of the purported teachings, deeds, sayings, silent approvals, silent disapprovals, habits, and practices of Muhammad. Sunnah means "a path; a way; a manner of life." In other words, the Sunnah contains all the alleged traditions and practices of the prophet and is the model that all Muslims should follow. His practices are to be adhered to in order to fulfill the divine injunctions, follow the religious rites, and mold one's life in accord with the will of Allah.

Sirah

Sirah means "to travel" or "be on a journey." The sirah is "The Life of Muhammad." In the first two centuries after the death of Muhammad, the stories of the prophet circulated, particularly of his military expeditions. *(8)* Muhammad was said to have allegedly led seventy-seven military expeditions. The earliest biography of the prophet is believed to have been written by Muhammad Ibn Ishaq, who recited his stories of the prophet to his students. His biography no longer exists, but his stories of Muhammad were probably used by other biographers. Muhammad Ibn Ishaq died somewhere between AD 770 and 772.

One critic has said that there are many discrepancies in the various sirahs. He goes on to say that parts dealing with the miracles Muhammad performed are not "fit sources of historical information" and that embellishments and exaggerations are common to storytelling.

(1) **Islam by Caesar Farah, pages 97–100**
(2) **Islam by Caesar Farah, pages 95**
(3) **Ibn Al-Rawandi, (AD 827-911); fragments from his writings contained in *The Book of the Emerald*, page 30**
(4) **Crone & Cook, 11977.18 (internet)**
(5) **Matt Slick (internet)**
(6) ***The Truth About Muhammad* by Robert Spencer, page 30**
(7) **Wikipedia**
(8) **"Maghazi" or stories of Muhammad's military expeditions.**

CHAPTER 6

ISLAM

Islam: *"to surrender"*; Surrender to the one and only God, Allah.

It is important in understanding present-day Islam to examine its theology. I have chosen several common subjects and practices that should provide you with a basic knowledge of Islam. It must be emphasized that each Muslim country will vary in what they practice and believe. And, like Judaism and Christianity, there are denominations within Islam that also have their own belief system and theologies. Islam is the way of life for those who believe in God and want to live a life of worship and obedience to none but God. The reward is forgiveness from God and an everlasting life in the Heaven.

Belief in one God, *Allah* in Arabic, constitutes the very foundation of Islam. There is no deity except Allah. He is indivisible and absolutely transcendent. God is the Almighty—the Creator and the Sustainer of the universe—who is similar to nothing, and nothing is comparable to Him. Worship and obedience belong to Allah and Allah alone. Joining other gods with God is an unforgivable sin. Anyone who joins other gods with God has strayed far away from the truth.

Prophet Muhammad was born in Mecca, a city in present-day Saudi Arabia in AD 570. He is a direct descendant of Prophet Ishmael, the first son of Prophet Abraham. Muhammad received divine revelations

(The Holy Koran) over a period of twenty-three years in the seventh century of the Christian Era. Muslims believe that he was the last Messenger sent by God for the guidance of mankind until the Day of Judgment. He is the model for humanity of all walks of life to follow until the Last Judgment. God sent him to bring mercy for the worlds.

The Koran is the Divine Book revealed to Muhammad. It confirms what was earlier revealed to the prophets or messengers of Allah and is the only source of guidance from Allah for all mankind. In addition to the Koran, another main source is the Sunnah, which includes the teachings and actions in the life of Muhammad. Anyone wanting to live a life in obedience to Allah must follow these teachings.

Belief that all the books of the prophets were given to them by Allah. This includes the Torah (Book of Moses), the Zabur (The Book of David), the Injeel ((Gospel of Jesus), and the Koran. However, the Koran is the only divine book in existence today in the original revealed form.

The Basic Concepts of Islamic Theology

Allah: Following the Judeo-Christian affirmation regarding Allah, Islam teaches that there is only One God who is Eternal and Supreme, Almighty and Infinite, Merciful and Compassionate, Generous and Forgiving, and Creator and Provider. To the Muslim, this belief requires complete trust and hope in Allah, submission to His Will, and reliance on His support. This submission secures man's dignity and saves him from fear and despair, from guilt and confusion. Since Allah is the creator of everything, he is also the guardian over everything, and to him belongs the keys to the heavens and earth.

Allah's Messengers: Islam teaches that all the messengers of Allah are equal. These messengers were great teachers of righteousness. They were chosen by Allah to teach mankind and deliver his divine message. They were sent at different times throughout history, and every nation had one messenger or more. The Koran mentions the names of twenty-five of them, and the Muslim believes in them all and accepts them as authorized messengers of Allah. They were, with the exception of Muhammad, known as "national" or local messengers. Their message and their religion had the same purpose, which was to guide humanity to Allah. All the messengers, including Jesus, were human beings given revelations and appointed by Allah to perform certain tasks. The names of some of the great messengers: Noah, Abraham, Ishmael, Moses, Jesus, and Muhammad. However, Islam claims Muhammad stands as The Last and Greatest Messenger.

Scriptures and Revelations:

Islam teaches that all the scriptures and revelations were from Allah. They were the guide the messengers received to show their respective peoples the right path of God. In the Koran, a special reference is made to the books of Abraham, Moses, David, and Jesus.

Angels: Islam teaches that the angels of Allah are spiritual beings who require no food or drink or sleep. They have no physical desires of any kind, nor any material needs. They spend their days and nights in the service of Allah. There are many angels, and each one is charged with a certain duty.

Creation: Life has purpose beyond the physical needs and material activities of man. The purpose of man is to worship Allah. To worship Allah is to know him; to love him; to obey his commandments; to enforce his law in every aspect of life; to serve his cause by doing the right and rejecting the evil; and to be just in our dealings with our fellow human beings.

When Allah charges man with any responsibility, he provides him with all the required assistance. He endows him with intelligence and power to choose his course of conduct. Man, thus, is commended by Allah to exert his utmost to fully serve the purpose of his existence. Should he fail to do that, or should he misuse his life or neglect his duties, he shall be responsible to God for his wrong deeds. Therefore, man has the responsibility to serve Allah's purpose on earth.

Born a Muslim: Islam teaches that every person is born "Muslim." This apparently means that, at birth, Allah has pre-engineered in each person the potential to realize His plans and submit to His will, which can make each person a Muslim...*if* they have access to Islam. Islam declares that it is the only universal and true religion of Allah.

Born Free from Sin: Islam teaches that every person is born free from sin. He is a blank ledger. But when the person reaches the age of maturity, he becomes accountable for his deeds and intentions. Man is not only free from sin until he commits sin, but he is also free to do things according to his plans. This dual freedom from sin and freedom to do good deeds clears his conscience from the pressure of inherited original sin. Islam does not believe that man is born with Adam's Original Sin.

Salvation: Islam teaches that man must work out his salvation through the guidance of Allah. This means that in order to attain salvation, a person must combine faith and action. Faith without action is as insufficient as action without faith. In other words, no one can attain salvation until his faith in Allah becomes dynamic in his life and his beliefs are translated into proper, acceptable actions. Allah does not accept lip service and no true believer can be indifferent as far as the requirements of faith are concerned. It also declares that no one can act on behalf of another or intercede between him and Allah.

Knowing the Right Way: Islam teaches that Allah does not hold any person responsible until He has shown him the right way. This is the reason Allah has sent many messengers and revelations and has made it clear that there would be no punishment prior to providing guidance. Therefore, a person who has never come across any Divine revelations or messenger, or is an insane person, is not held responsible to Allah for failing to obey the Divine instructions. Such a person will be responsible only for not doing what his common sense tells him to do. But the person who knowingly and intentionally violates the Law of Allah or deviates from His right path will be punished for his wrong deeds.

Human Nature: Islam teaches that in human nature, there is more good than evil, and the probability of successful reform is greater than the probability of hopeless failure. Islam teaches that faith is not complete when it is followed blindly or accepted unquestioningly. If faith is to inspire action, and if faith and action are to lead to salvation, then faith must be founded on unshakable convictions without any compulsion. If the person is not certain about his faith, he is to use his reasoning powers to reflect on the teachings of the Koran. He must search for the truth until he finds it, and he will certainly find it if he is capable and serious enough. (To Christians, this is known as "working out your own salvation.")

The Words of Allah: Islam teaches that the Koran contains the very words of Allah revealed to Muhammad through the Angel Gabriel. The Koran was revealed by Allah on various occasions to answer certain questions, solve certain problems, settle certain disputes, and to be man's guide to the truth of Allah and eternal happiness. For Islam, every word in the Koran is from Allah, and every sound in it is the true echo of Allah's voice. The Koran is the first and most authentic source of Islam. It was revealed in Arabic. It is still and will remain in its original and complete Arabic version, because Allah has made it His concern to preserve the Koran, to make it always the best guide for man, and to safeguard it against corruption. (Therefore, Allah only speaks and listens to people in the Arabic language.)

The Koran and the Traditions of Muhammad: Islam teaches that there is a clear distinction between the Koran and the Traditions of Muhammad. The Koran is the word of Allah, whereas the Traditions of Muhammad are the practical interpretations of Muhammad's actions and decisions. The role of Muhammad was to convey the Koran as he received it, to interpret it, and to practice it fully. His interpretations and practices produced what is known as the Traditions of Muhammad. They are considered the second source of Islam and must be in complete harmony with the first source, namely, the Koran. If there are any contradictions or inconsistencies between any of the Traditions and the Koran, the Muslim adheres to the Koran and regards everything else as open to question because no genuine Tradition of Muhammad can ever disagree with the Koran.

The Day of Judgment: Islam teaches that there is the Last Judgment Day. This world will come to an end and the dead will rise to stand before Allah to be judged. Everything in life has been accurately recorded—every action, intention, thought, and word. People with good records will be rewarded and welcomed into heaven. Those with bad records will be punished and cast into hell.

Salvation and the Afterlife:

The basic criterion for salvation in the afterlife is the belief in One God, the Last Judgment, good deeds, the messengers of God, Allah's angels, and that Muhammad was the final prophet of God. But salvation can only be attained through God's judgment.

"Did ye think that ye would enter Heaven without Allah testing those of you who fought hard (in His cause) and remained steadfast?" Koran 3:142

Conditions of Going to Paradise According to the Koran:

> *Those who spend (freely), whether in prosperity, or in adversity; who restrain (their) anger, and pardon (all) men; for Allah loves those who do good (to others). And those who, having done something to be ashamed of, or wronged their own souls, do earnestly bring Allah to mind and ask for forgiveness for their sins, and do not knowingly persist in (the wrong)*

they have done. For such, is the reward of forgiveness from their Lord, and Gardens with rivers flowing underneath, will have an eternal dwelling for their reward of their labors. —Koran 3:134–137

Allah did aforetime take a covenant from the Children of Israel, and we appointed twelve captains among them. And Allah said: "I am with you: if ye (but) establish regular prayers, practice regular charity, believe in my messengers, honor and assist them, and offer to Allah a beautiful gift, verily I will wipe out from you your evil deeds, and admit you to Gardens with rivers flowing beneath; but if any of you, after this, resists the faith, he hath truly wandered from the path shall indeed lose the right way. —Koran 5:12

As in life, there are many trials one must face. This is also a condition that individuals must encounter in order to enter Paradise (**Jannah**: Heaven, Paradise, Gardens).

Or do ye think that ye shall enter the Garden (of bliss) without such (trials) as came to those who passed away before you? They encountered suffering and adversity, and were so shaken in spirit that even the Messenger and those of faith who were with him cried: 'When (will come) the help of Allah?' Ah! Verily, the help of Allah is (always) near. —Koran 2:214

The Koran also asserts that those who reject the prophets of God with their best knowledge are damned in the afterlife, and if they reject in front of the Messenger of God, then they also face a dreadful fate in this world and in the afterlife. Conversely, a person who discovers monotheism without having been reached by a messenger is called *Hanif*. Hanifs include Jews, Christians, and any of the religions who believe in *one* God.

Jannah (Heaven): According to hadith, there are eight doors of Heaven. Their names are as follows:

1. For those who were punctual in prayer.
2. For those who took part in jihad.
3. For those who gave charity more often.
4. For those who fasted.
5. For those participated in the annual pilgrimage.
6. For those who withheld their anger and forgave others.
7. For those who by virtue of their faith are saved from reckoning and chastisement.
8. For those who showed zeal in remembering God.

Names for Heaven: _____

The Highest Gardens of the Paradise

The Home

Home of Peace

The Home in the Hereafter

Gardens of Everlasting Bliss

The Eternal Gardens

Garden of Abode

The Gardens of Delight

Assembly of Truth

The House of Security

General Practices and Teachings

Mosques: *(1)* Muhammad's place of prayer in Medina became the prototype for Mosques: clay walls surrounding a spacious courtyard. It was not only the place of prayer but also used as the social and political center for the original community of believers. The early mosques often included:

- The seat of government
- The administration of justice
- Delivery of sermons
- Political gatherings
- Proclamation of military orders
- Sealing of business deals
- Marriage terms agreed upon
- Shelter and rest stop
- Asylum for poor travelers and the persecuted

Some mosques were adapted for use as hospitals; kitchens for the poor; nursing homes; and living quarters for pious ascetics to study Islam. Mosques were *not* considered "houses of Allah."

- No images were permitted
- No altars
- No mystic or ritual activities

The <u>primary purpose</u> of mosques was for communal prayer ritual, particularly on Fridays. There was no special ceremony for the Mosques' consecration, but it had to be set apart from "unclean" daily activities. However, any place could serve as a place of prayer. For intimate conversations with Allah, any small free space is sufficient, providing that the person is facing the Kaaba in Mecca *(2)* and that the spot is clean (usually a small rug for kneeling). Nevertheless, it is considered "worthy" to pray in a mosque. Domed mosques were a later development of the Ottoman Empire in the fourteenth century.

Today, most mosques generally provide:

- A place for religious washing
- A minaret tower, which issues the call to worship five times a day
- A semicircular niche, which indicates the direction of the Kaaba in Mecca
- A platform or pulpit where the prayer leader (**Imam**) delivers his sermon *(3)*

Shoes are not permitted in the main area of the mosque. After the removal of the shoes, the necessary preliminary for prayer involves washing for the purpose of purification or "ablution." Ritual washing involves the hands, head, forearms, and feet. In addition, the rinsing out the mouth, the blowing out of the nose, and the scrubbing out of the ears is also advisable. When no water is available, the Koran allows the believer to "dry wash" using sand or a pebble. *(4)*

The prayers are conducted in the mosque at noon on Fridays (Friday being their holy day of the week). The weekly sermon is delivered, which not only involves religious matters but also raises social and political issues. The prayer service opens with all believers standing in straight rows with heads covered, facing Mecca. The Imam announces that "prayer is ready." Various positions and movements are taken throughout the act of praying. In one of the final acts of praying, the prayer falls to his knees twice, touching his forehead on the floor (or ground) to symbolize his total devotion and subjection to Allah, saying *"**Allah Akbar**,"* meaning, "Allah is the Greatest!" *(5)*

Prayers: Every prayer is composed of several cycles of movements, and at the conclusion of cycles, the prayer of affirms at the end, *"There is no god but Allah; Muhammad is his messenger."* Finally, turning the head to the right and left, he offers the greeting to his neighbors saying, *"Peace and the mercy of Allah be with you."*

Prayer "or Worry" Beads: *(6)* The Muslims adopted the early Christian monks' devotional beads used to recite or pray the Lord's Prayer thirty-three times. The Muslim moves the beads rhythmically between his thumb and index finger so that one bead clicks against another. Each bead represents a name of Allah. There are thirty- three beads, which require the cycle to be repeated three times for the ninety-nine names of Allah.

Marriage: Marriage is held in high esteem by the Koran. But it is not considered a solemn, festive act by which the bride and groom impose high moral obligations upon each other, and it is rarely performed in a mosque. Legally, marriage is a contract and therefore a matter of a civil law, which is usually settled privately or in the office of a judge *(7)*.

The Ceremony: The ceremony includes a public declaration of the bride's agreement and a statement of the amount of the dowry, *(8)* of which she receives a portion immediately with the rest set aside in case of a divorce. The bride does not have to appear personally; an authorized male representative acts in her stead. When agreement to the contract is reached, those present recite together the first chapter of the Koran to strengthen the contract. The festivities before and following the marriage contract vary according to region and may last up to a week. The feast is held in the house of the bride, at which both families (or even clans) gather. The poor are supposed to be invited, and money is thrown to them. Before the meal, the bride bathes with her friends and then is elaborately adorned. The groom rides through the streets with friends. On the fourth day, the bride proceeds (sometimes on a litter) in a festive procession to the house of the groom where she receives blessings and best wishes for her happiness. The celebration of the marriage ceremony concludes with the couple's first mutual bath and the reception of visitors in their new home.

Women: Islam believes that Allah created women to be subordinate and inferior to men. This gives men authority over women. Husbands are given the authority to discipline and punish their wives. Men are, however, required to treat women fairly. A woman's role is to serve men's needs. Women should:

- Usually be veiled in public, so no flesh is showing
- Not eat with men
- Walk four paces behind the man

Divorce: *(9)* The husband can unilaterally demand a divorce by repeating "*I divorce you*" three times after a waiting period of three menstrual periods and carry through with the divorce. A man may divorce his wife three times, taking her back after the first two (reconciling). After the third divorce, they can't get back together until she marries someone else. Some do a "triple divorce" in which the man says in one sitting "*I divorce you*" three times (or "*I divorce you, three times,*" "*you're triple divorced*"). Many Islamic scholars believe there is a waiting period involved between the three divorces, pointing to the Koran and various hadiths. However, the practice of "triple divorce" at one sitting has been legally recognized historically and has been particularly practiced in Saudi Arabia.

Shia and Sunni Muslims have different rules for performing a divorce. According to some Sunni schools of jurisprudence, each divorce utterance should be followed by a waiting period of three menstrual periods for the woman or three months, *(10)* at which point the couple is supposed to try to reconcile with the help of mediators from each family until the third and final divorce. Some Sunnis who believe the practice of triple divorce is wrong accept it as final nonetheless.

Shias don't have the concept of verbal "Triple Divorce," i.e. uttering the phrase "*I divorce you*" three times. The Shi'a practice also dictates a three-month waiting period when the couple is supposed to try to reconcile with the help of mediators from each family but requires two witnesses for the declaration of the divorce. If the couple breaks the waiting period, the divorce is voided. After the waiting period is over, the couple is divorced, and the husband is no longer responsible for the wife's expenses but remains responsible for the maintenance of the children until they are weaned.

It is also possible for a woman to petition a judge of Muslim jurisprudence *(11)* for a divorce under certain conditions. The circumstances regarded as acceptable vary amongst the four Sunni groups of Islamic schools of jurisprudence. In certain Muslim countries, the divorced wife retains all girls and the boys until age seven, thereafter the father assumes responsibility of the boys while the girls stay with the mother.

Alimony: The husband pays alimony in accordance with his wife's lifestyle until the divorce is finalized. The wife retains her dowry and any accumulation of jewelry and other monies acquired during her marriage.

Birth of a Child: As soon as the umbilical cord of a newborn child is cut, the call to prayer is whispered into the child's right ear, and the second call to prayer is whispered into the left ear. Seven days later, the infant is given its name in the presence of relatives and friends of the family. The baby's head is shaved for seven days after birth, and one or two goats are slaughtered, depending on whether the baby is a boy or girl.

Circumcision: Circumcision is observed differently according to individual countries and legal schools. The Koran makes no mention of it. However, it is considered an indispensable ritual of purification and an indelible sign of membership in the Muslim Community. It is performed between the seventh and fourteenth day after birth.

Circumcision of girls was a custom stemming from pre-Islamic times. It was justified as necessary to curb female sexuality, and it is still practiced among certain Muslim tribes in Africa. According to the Islamic religion, it is neither required nor recommended.

Suffering: Illness, suffering, and dying are considered part of life and a **test** from God. Suffering serves two purposes:

1) a form of punishment;
2) a form of test or trial.

Death: Death is nothing more than part of a journey and transformation from one life to another and a component of faith.

Day of Judgment: Human life in this world constitutes a trial—an examination period during which the Muslim prepares him/herself for either good or ill in the next life of indefinite duration. On that day, "... *every soul shall be paid back in full what it has earned, and they shall not be dealt with unjustly.*" *(9)* On the Day of Judgment, the bodies of the dead will be raised and rejoined with their souls to stand before God and give an accounting. Judgment to Heaven or to the burning fires of Hell will be enjoyed or endured in physical form by the new bodies God will raise.

Day of Judgment of Nations: The Koran recognizes another kind of Divine Judgment, which is meted out in history to nations, peoples, and communities who have been corrupted by wealth or subjugated by more virtuous nations.

Funerals: According to Islamic law, a dead body should be buried as soon as possible from the time of death, which means funeral planning and preparations begin immediately. Routine autopsies are not acceptable in Islam, as they are seen as a desecration of the body. Embalming and cosmetology are not allowed unless required by state or federal law. Funeral procedures begin with the removal of clothing, followed by washing the body (the ritual of ablution) by members of the immediate family if possible. (If there are any missing body parts, they are sought out so they can be buried with the body.) All bodily openings are stuffed with cotton to prevent evil spirits from entering.

The body is then wrapped in a seamless, light- colored cloth with those present reciting from the Koran.

The deceased is taken to the mosque. There, prayers for the dead are recited, and family and friends are obligated to attend. The deceased is carried to the cemetery in procession. Traditionally, only men are allowed to be present at the burial. However, in some Islamic communities, all mourners, including women, are allowed at the gravesite. The grave is supposed to be dug perpendicular to the position of prayer and the body placed in the grave on its right side *(10)*. Those placing the body into the grave should recite, *"In the name of Allah and in the faith of the Messenger of Allah."*

Once the body is in the grave, a layer of wood or stones is placed on top of the body to prevent direct contact between the body and the soil that will fill the grave. Then each mourner present places three handfuls of soil into the grave. Once the grave has been filled, a small stone or marker may be placed at the grave so that it is recognizable. However, it is prohibited to erect a large monument on the grave or decorate the grave in any elaborate way. After the funeral and burial, the immediate family gathers and receives visitors. It is customary for the community to provide food for the family for the first few days of the mourning period. Generally, the mourning period lasts forty days, but depending on how strictly the family chooses to follow custom, the mourning period may be much shorter.

Hospitality: It is an Islamic obligation—whatever one's station in life—to show hospitality is an expression of righteousness. Hospitality is shown regardless of personal cost and is expected in return. Failure to show hospitality is inexcusable. It applies not only to the home but also to chance encounters. The guest or guests are treated with respect and honor and provided with food, water for their feet, rest, and a sumptuous feast. Rules for hospitality include—

-   Do not cross legs so that you show the bottom of shoes
-   Do not eat with left hand; it is considered the hand used for toilet needs

- Do not ask the host about his wife
- Do not show host pictures of women with arms or legs uncovered (which is equivalent to pornography)
- Women that are covered may mingle with the men

Other Meaningful Procedures and Practices

Dietary Practices: Pork is a forbidden food. Animals must be slaughtered by cutting their throats and draining the blood. Milk from animals used for food is forbidden. Alcoholic beverages are forbidden. Gluttony and over-indulgences are discouraged. In an emergency, however, anything edible is lawful.

Dignity: A person's dignity, honor, and reputation are of paramount importance, and no effort is spared to protect them. Muslims pride themselves on generosity, humanitarianism, politeness, and loyalty, which they believe distinguishes themselves from non-Muslims.

Bargaining: Bargaining is a respected part of business procedures, and shopkeepers expect one to take the time to participate in the ceremony and social exchange associated with buying. However, arguing demeans the object. Shopkeepers respect knowledge, skill, and wit.

Blue and the Evil Eye: The color blue is associated with magical powers. People with blue eyes are believed to have the power to employ the "evil eye." The color blue is also thought to ward off the evil eye. The evil eye is a common belief that individuals have the power to look at people, animals, or objects to cause them harm.

Open Hand: The raised open hand is a powerful sign of good luck and is able to overcome the evil eye.

Green: The color green is the "holy" color of Islam. The prophet's cloak was said to have been green.

<u>Beards</u>: Beards are considered the symbol of a man's dignity.

<u>Mustaches</u>: Mustaches are a symbol of a Muslim's virility, masculinity, dignity, and strength. When a Muslim strokes his mustache in connection with an oath or promise, it is a sign of his sincerity. It is an insult to touch or verbally denigrate a Muslim's mustache.

(1) **Masjid: A place of prostration**
(2) **Mihrab: The niche in the wall of the mosque indicating the direction of Mecca**
(3) **Minhar: The pulpit where the prayer leader (Imam) delivers sermons**
(4) **Wudu: Ritual washing in preparation for prayers**
(5) **Shahahah: "There is no god but Allah; Muhammad is his messenger."**
(6) **Mishaha: Muslim prayer beads**
(7) **Qadi: A judge who reviews civil, judicial, and religious matters according to Islamic law.**
(8) **Mahr: A mandatory payment in the form of money or possessions paid or promised to be paid by the groom or by the groom's father to the bride at the time of** marriage, **which legally becomes her property. While the mahr is often money, it can also be anything agreed upon by the bride such as jewelry, home goods, furniture, a dwelling, or some land. Mahr is typically specified in the marriage contract signed during or before an Islamic marriage.**
(9) **Talaq: "Divorce;" "I divorce you." (Koran 65)**
(10) **Iddah: three-month waiting period; three menstrual periods**
(11) **Qadi: Judge of Muslim jurisprudence**

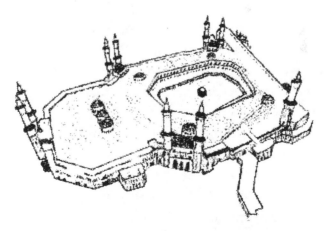

***Masjid al-Haram* (The Sacred Mosque)** *in Mecca*
Also called "Grand Mosque or Great Mosque of Mecca

CHAPTER 7

ISLAMIC LAW

Sharia Law: The meaning of *sharia* has its roots in the Semitic word "sara," which is interpreted as "way" or "path." The term evolved into the Arabic word denoting "pathway to be followed" or "path to the water hole." This latter definition comes from the fact that the path to water is the necessary manner of survival in a desert environment. To the Muslim, sharia law is a body of moral and religious laws derived from religious sacred writings, as opposed to human legislation, and is the "pathway" to arrive in the Heavens after the Day of Judgment.

Origins of Sharia Law: Sharia is considered by Islam to be the "Divine Law" as expressed in the Koran and the traditions gathered from the life of Muhammad, his actions, and his words. The formative period of the sharia stretches back to the time of the early Muslim communities, at which time many problems and questions were brought to the attention of Muhammad's closest comrades for consultation. During this period, they were more concerned with pragmatic issues of authority and teaching. In the 660s, questions began to be raised that were not originally covered by Islamic law. In response, the Caliph began appointing Islamic judges *(1)*. The jurisdiction of the judges only included Muslims. During the "Islamic Golden Age" (from the seventh to the thirteenth century), a number of legal concepts and institutions were developed by Islamic jurists.

From the ninth century onward, the power to interpret the law in traditional Islamic societies was in the hands of the scholars. This separation of powers served to limit the range of actions available to the ruler, who could not easily decree or reinterpret law independently and still expect the continued support of the community. Through succeeding centuries and empires, the balance between Muslim scholars and rulers shifted and reformed, but the balance of power was never decisively changed.

Over the course of many centuries of imperial, political and technological change—including the Industrial Revolution and the French Revolution—a new era of European control and influence was ushered in that gradually included the domination of many of the lands previously ruled by Islamic empires.

At the end of the Second World War, the European powers found themselves too weakened to maintain their empires as before. The wide variety of forms of government, systems of law, attitudes toward modernity, and interpretations of sharia are a result of the ensuing drives for independence and modernity in the Muslim world. According to Jan Michiel Otto, Professor of Law and Governance in Developing Countries at Leiden University,

> *Anthropological research shows that people in local communities often do not distinguish clearly whether and to what extent their norms and practices are based on local tradition, tribal custom, or religion. Those who adhere to a confrontational view of sharia tend to ascribe many undesirable practices to sharia and religion, overlooking custom and culture, even if high- ranking religious authorities have stated the opposite. (2)*

Sharia law is a very diverse and complicated set of rules and guidelines. Some scholars have pointed out that the sharia is not formally a code or a well-defined set of rules. The sharia is characterized as a "discussion" on the duties of Muslims based on the opinion of the Muslim community and extensive literature.

Countries with Muslim Majority: Most countries with a Muslim majority incorporate sharia at some level in their legal framework, with many calling it the "highest law" or the "source of law of the land" in their constitutions. Most use sharia for personal law (marriage, divorce, domestic violence, child support, family law, inheritance, and such matters). Elements of sharia are present, to varying extents, in the criminal justice system of many Muslim majority countries. Saudi Arabia, Yemen, Brunei, Qatar, Pakistan, the United Arab Emirates, Iraq, Afghanistan, and Mauritania apply the code predominantly while Indonesia applies it partially.

Penalties and Punishment: Most Muslim-majority countries with sharia law prescribe harsh punishments in their legal code, but sometimes use other punishments instead. The harshest sharia penalties, such as stoning, beheadings, limb removal, and the death penalty, are enforced with varying levels of consistency. Since the 1970s, most Muslim-majority countries have faced strong demands from their religious groups and political parties for immediate adoption of sharia law as their sole or at least primary legal framework. Some moderates and liberal scholars within these Muslim countries have argued for limited expansion of sharia law.

The Range of Sharia Law: The extent of the sharia law includes:

- Hygiene and purification laws (procedures for religious cleansing)
- Economic laws (alms giving, interest rates, and inheritance)
- Dietary laws (ritual slaughter of appropriate animals for sacrifice or food (*Halal*)
- Religious obligations (hajj, prayers, celebrations, and feasts)
- Personal status laws (marriage contracts, divorce, and child custody)

- Criminal law (fixed punishment, discretionary punishment, retaliation, blood money *(3)*, and apostasy)
- Military law (truces and rules regarding prisoners of war)
- Dress codes (women dress in burkas in public)

Women's Rights: Sharia law grants women the right to inherit property from family members, but a woman's inheritance is less that a man's and is equal to half of the inheritance her brother receives. Child marriages are common in the Middle Eastern countries, accounting for an average of about one in six marriages, depending on the country.

Enforcement of Sharia Law: Various Islamic nations enforce sharia law in differing ways and means. Saudi Arabia, for example, employs a government-authorized religious police *(4)*.

The Islamic doctrine of "accountability"*(5)* states that it is the religious obligation of every Muslim to report to the authorities any wrong behavior of a neighbor, relative, or stranger that violates sharia law or in any way insults Islam. The authority (or authorities) then has a divine responsibility to take appropriate action. In the modern age, this doctrine has been used in several Muslim-majority countries to enforce sharia restrictions on blasphemy and criticism of Islam over the internet and social media.

Judicial Proceedings: Sharia courts usually do not rely on lawyers. Trials are conducted solely by the judge, and there is no jury. Plaintiffs and defendants represent themselves. Judges' verdicts do not set binding precedents. Male Muslim witnesses are considered more reliable than female Muslim witnesses, and non-Muslim witnesses are considered unreliable. In criminal cases in more conservative Muslim-majority countries, female witnesses are unacceptable.

Criminal Cases: In sharia courts where religious crimes are tried—such as accusing someone of illicit sex without proof, apostasy, drinking alcohol, and theft—the testimony of Muslim witnesses serves as the main source of admissible evidence. Neither forensic evidence nor circumstantial evidence is admissible. At least two Muslim male witnesses, or one Muslim male and two Muslim females who are not related to one another and are of sound mind and reliable character, may provide testimony. To try crimes of adultery, fornication, or rape, there must be four Muslim male witnesses. Some jurists allow the substitution of up to three male witnesses and six female witnesses. Muslim jurists have debated whether coerced confessions or coerced witnesses are acceptable. (In the **Ottoman Criminal Code**, officials were allowed to use torture only if the accused had a bad reputation and there was indication or evidence of guilt.)

Civil Cases: Civil cases involve the following types of contracts:

- Debt-related transactions
- Oral contracts for commercial and other civil contracts
- Marriage contracts relating to the dowry

Court Cases: Sharia courts treat women and men as unequal, with a Muslim woman's compensation equal to half that of a Muslim man. In cases where a Jewish or a Christian male plaintiff wins the case, they are awarded fifty percent of that of a Muslim man, and other non-Muslims (Buddhists, Hindus, Jains, and atheists) are only entitled to one-sixteenth of the amount a male Muslim would receive. The Human Rights Watch and the annual report by the United States Commission on International Religious Freedom note that in the sharia courts of Saudi Arabia, "The calculation of accidental death or injury compensation is discriminatory."

Rules for Conversion to Islam: Accordinaw, the guidelines for religious conversion under sharia law are:

> If a person converts to Islam or is born and raised a Muslim, then he or she will have full rights of citizenship in an Islamic state.

Leaving Islam is a sin and a religious crime. Any man or woman who is a Muslim will be subject to the death penalty if he or she abandons the Islamic religion. Before execution, sharia demands that the individual be offered one chance to return to Islam.

If a person has never been a Muslim and is not an infidel or unbeliever, sharia law demands that they can live in an Islamic state by accepting to become a *"protected person"* with certain limitations of rights as a subject of an Islamic state and without legal equality with Muslims.

If a person is an infidel, sharia law demands that they convert to Islam, become a protected person, or be enslaved, killed, or ransomed.

Other Examples of the Intrusive and Restrictive Sharia Law:

- Criticizing or denying any part of the Koran is punishable by death (the Koran *is* Allah's word).
- Criticizing Muhammad, denying that he is a prophet, or drawing a caricature of him is punishable by death.
- Criticizing or denying that Allah is God is punishable by death.
- The act of a non-Muslim leading a Muslim away from Islam is punishable by death.
- A man can marry an infant girl and consummate the marriage.
- Girls' clitorises should be removed (Book 41, Kitab Al- Adab, Hadith 5,251).
- A woman can have one husband who can have up to four wives or more if he a caliph (harem).
- A man can beat his wife for insubordination.
- A man can unilaterally divorce his wife, but a woman needs her husband's consent to divorce.

- A divorced wife loses custody of male children when they reach seven years of age.
- A woman who has been raped cannot testify in court against her rapist(s).
- A woman cannot drive a car, as it leads to upheaval and chaos (*fitnah*).
- A woman cannot speak alone to a man who is not her husband or relative.
- Meat must come from animals that have been sacrificed to Allah (*Halal*).
- Muslims should engage in dishonesty to non-Muslims to advance the cause of Islam.

Fundamentalists: We have already mentioned in other chapters the desire of various extremists groups within Islam whose goal is to return to basic religious Islamic values and laws. They have practiced jihad to impose sharia punishments for crimes, have curtailed civil rights, and have violated human rights. They have used the Koran and the rigid interpretation of sharia law to justify acts of war and terror—not only against non-Muslims but against their fellow Muslims—in order to establish a Caliphate and universalize Islam. The basic philosophy is that "peace will come after all other religions submit to sharia law."

With growing Muslim immigrant communities in Europe, there have been reports in some media of "no-go zones" being established where sharia law reigns supreme and where Muslim men and youth gangs are molesting non-Muslim women and calling them whores.

Freedom of Thought, Conscience and Religion: Sharia law has been criticized by the United Nations' Declaration of Human Rights because it does not recognize their declaration that *". . . every human has the right to freedom of thought, conscience and religion; this right includes freedom to change their religion or belief."* In the United States, sixteen States have introduced legislation to ban sharia law.

(1) *Qadis*: Islamic judges.
(2) Otto's analysis appears in a paper commissioned by the Netherlands Ministry of Foreign Affairs.
(3) *Diyya*: the financial compensation paid to the victim or heirs of a victim in the cases of murder, bodily harm, or property damage.
(4) *Mutaween*: religious police
(5) *Hisbah*: accountability

CHAPTER 8

JIHAD

The word *jihad* appears frequently in the Koran, often to express "striving in the way of Allah," referring to the act of striving to serve the purposes of Allah on this earth. In Arabic, the word jihad is a noun meaning the act of "striving and applying oneself, struggling, or persevering." However, Muslim scholars do not all agree on this definition. Muslims and non-Muslims alike suggest that jihad as having two meanings:

The inner spiritual struggle (the "greater jihad")

The outer physical struggle against the enemies of Islam (the "lesser jihad"), which may take a violent or nonviolent form. Jihad is often translated as "Holy War," although this term is controversial.

According to Bernard Lewis, "the overwhelming majority of classical theologians, jurists," and specialists in the hadith "understood the obligation of jihad in a military sense." Javed Ahmad Ghamidi, a well-known Pakistani theologian, states that there is a consensus among Islamic scholars that the concept of jihad will always include armed struggle against wrongdoers. Jihad is sometimes referred to as the sixth pillar of Islam, although it occupies no such official status. In Twelver Shi'a Islam, however, jihad is one of the ten Practices of the Religion *(1)*.

What does the Koran Say about jihad? *(2)*

And fight in the way of Allah with those who fight with you, and do not exceed the limits, surely Allah does not love those who exceed the limits. And kill them wherever you find them, and drive them out from whence they drove you out, and persecution is severer than slaughter, and do not fight them at the Sacred Mosque until they fight with you in it, but if they do not fight you, they slay them; such is the recompense of the unbelievers. But if they desist, then surely Allah is Forgiving, Merciful. And fight with them until there is no persecution, and religion should be only for Allah. But if they desist, then there should be no hostility except against the oppressors.

—Koran 2: 190–193

Therefore let those fight in the way of Allah, who sell this world's life for the hereafter; and whoever fights in the way of Allah, then be he slain or be he victorious, we shall grant him a mighty reward. And what reason have you that you should not fight in the way of Allah and of the weak among the men and the women and the children, (of) those who say: Our Lord! Cause us to go forth from this town, whose people are oppressors, and give us from Thee a guardian and give us from Thee a helper. Those who believe fight in the way of Allah, and those who disbelieve fight in the way of the Shaitan (Satan); surely the strategy of the Shaitan (Satan) is weak.

—Koran 4:74–76

When your Lord revealed to the angels: I am with you, therefore make firm those who believe. I will cast terror into the hearts of those who disbelieve. Therefore strike off heads and strike off every fingertip of them.

—Koran 8:12

Say to those who disbelieve, if they desist, that which has past shall be forgiven to them; and if they return, then what happened to the ancients has already passed. And fight with them until there is no more persecution and religion should be only for Allah; but if they desist, then surely Allah sees what they do.

—Koran 8:38, 39

So when the sacred months have passed away, then slay the idolaters (other gods/pagans)* wherever you find them, and take them captive and besiege them and lie in wait for them every ambush, then if they repent and keep up prayer and pay the poor-rate, leave their way free to them; surely Allah is Forgiving, Merciful.

—Koran 9:5

* "Infidels" translator (Rodwell)

Fight those who do not believe in Allah, nor in the latter day, nor do they prohibit what Allah and His Apostle have prohibited, nor follow the religion of truth, out of those who have been given the Book, until they pay the tax in acknowledgment of superiority and they are in a state of subjection.

—*Koran 9:29*

So do not follow the unbelievers (infidels), and strive against them a mighty striving with it.

—*Koran 25:52*

Jihad *did not* Originate with Muhammad or the Koran: One of the cultural aspects of the Near (Middle) East people's early history is how religion and military wars were intertwined; that is, wars were religious wars, believed to be ordained by God. An example of this is the story from the Bible of Samuel, who was Israel's Judge, Prophet, and Priest. Responding to the people who were requesting a "King" who would lead them to victory over their enemies—the Amalekites and the Philistines—Samuel anointed Saul to be King and to lead the Israelite army to victory.

Samuel tells Saul, *"I am the one the Lord sent to anoint you king over his people Israel; so listen now to the message from the Lord. This is what the Lord Almighty says: 'I will punish the Amalekites for what they did to Israel when they waylaid them as they came up from Egypt. Now go, attack the Amalekites and totally destroy everything that belongs to them. Do not spare them; put to death men and women, children and infants, cattle and sheep, camels and donkeys."* (1 Samuel 15: 1–3, NIV)

This was a "holy" war because Samuel claims that God ordered or ordained it: jihad. The word "jihad" was not in the vocabulary at that time, but the concept of God ordaining war was a common cultural aspect of the peoples of that time and place.

Although the concept of jihad did not originate with Muhammad, he certainly practiced it against pagans, Jews, and Christians. Muhammad, like Samuel, became the interpreter of the will of God (Allah).

Muhammad combined the political power of a military leader, the religious power and the functions of a judge.

> ***Whosoever obeys the messenger (Muhammad), thereby obeys God.***
>
> **—Koran 4:82**
>
> ***The aim of jihad is to subjugate the peoples of the world to the law of Allah, decreed by his prophet Muhammad. . . . As the jihad is a permanent war, it excludes the idea of peace but authorizes temporary truces related to the political situation. Those truces must not last for more than ten years at the most and can be unilaterally denounced by the imam, after notifying the adversary. (3)***

Jihad by Hijrah:

> *"And whoever emigrates for the cause of Allah will find on the earth many locations and abundance, and whoever leaves his home as an emigrant to Allah and His Messenger and then death overtakes him, his reward has already become incumbent upon Allah."* (Koran 4:100)

Hijrah, or "jihad by emigration," is a concept that originates from the migration or escape of Muhammad and his followers from Mecca to Medina in the year 622. It was after the Hijrah that Muhammad, for the first time, became not just a preacher of religion but a political and military leader. That was what occasioned his new "revelations" exhorting his followers to commit violence against unbelievers. The

Islamic calendar counts the Hijrah— not Muhammad's birth or the occasion of his first revelation—as the beginning of Islam, implying that Islam is not fully realized without a political and military component.

When considering the current migrant crisis in the Middle East, one might wonder why Arab countries like Saudi Arabia, UAE, Oman, etc., aren't taking in refugees. The reason is that moving to a new land in order to bring Islam there is considered a holy and revered action. They are "missionaries" to convert their new country to the religion and laws of Islam.

Modern-Day Practice of Jihad: The 9/11/01 terrorist attack on the New York World Trade Center was an act of Jihad. "Muslims in Islamic-dominated countries rejoiced at the attack on the World Trade Center in New York. . . . (Islamists have) a loathing of modern society in general . . . and a more particularized loathing (and) fear of the prospect that their own immediate surroundings could be taken over—'*Westoxicate*'—by the liberal, Western-style way of life." *(4)*

In an article published on August 3, 2016, Dennis MacEoin stated that the West has allowed itself to be weakened by "A combination of political correctness, fear of giving offense, fear of combat, and a reluctance to upset illusory stability (which) has led to an incredible series of opportunities for the jihadists." He continues, "We have dropped our guard and turned away. Not because we have no security forces. We do. But because we often are not looking at the right things: the texts and sermons that prefigure radicalism."

It is alarming when people like the founder of the Muslim Brotherhood, Hassan al-Banna declares, "The Noble Quran appoints the Muslims as guardians over humanity in its minority, and grants them the rights of suzerainty *(5)* and dominion over the world in order to carry out this sublime commission. . . . We have come to the conclusion that it is our duty to establish sovereignty over the world and to guide all of humanity to the sound precepts of Islam and to its teachings. . . ."

Today's Terror Groups: This list is just the tip of the iceberg. There are many more, but these are the most prominent groups.

- **ISIL**: (The Islamic State of Iraq and the Levant). "The Levant" refers to all eastern Mediterranean countries and their islands.
- **ISIS**: (The Islamic State of Iraq and Syria)
- **Al-Qaeda**
- **Boko Haram**
- **Muslim Brotherhood**
- **Taliban**
- **Hamas**
- **Jamaat-i-Islami**
- **Kataib Hezbollah**

Who supports these terrorists? They are supported by oil money, kidnappings, ransom, and, according to reports, money from Saudi Arabia—the most fundamentally Islamic state and the wealthiest, most fertile ground for radical Islam. And what is the driving force that motivates Saudi Arabia to provide support for terrorism?

It is the **Wahhabi School of Islam.**

WAHHABISM

Wahhabism is named after an eighteenth-century Muslim scholar, Muhammad ibn Abd al-Wahhab (1703–1792). He started a movement advocating the purge of practices such as shrine and tomb visitation—which he considered idolatry (shirk)—impurities, and certain innovations in Islam. Eventually, he formed a pact with a local leader, offering political obedience and promising that protection and propagation of the Wahhabi movement would mean "power and glory" and the rule of "lands and men for him." The movement was centered on the principle of the "uniqueness" and "unity" of Allah. The movement also drew from the teachings of a medieval theologian and an early jurist.

Wahhabism today is a religious movement that works to bring Muslims back from what it believes are foreign interactions that have corrupted Islam. They believe that Islam is a complete way of life and therefore contains the prescriptions for *all* aspects of life. Wahhabism is extremely strict in what it considers Islamic behavior. As a result, it has been described as the strictest form of Sunni Islam.

The Wahhabi mission is to spread purified Islam through the world, both to Muslims and non-Muslims. The Saudi government and various charities have spent tens of billions of dollars on mosques, schools, education materials, and scholarships throughout the world to promote Islam and the Wahhabi interpretation of it.

Wahhabism is noted for its policy of compelling its own followers and other Muslims to strictly observe the religious duties of Islam, such as the five prayers, and for the enforcement of public morals to a degree not found elsewhere. While other Muslims might urge abstention from alcohol, modest dress, and prayer, for Wahhabis:

- Prayer must be punctual, ritually correct, and communally performed. It is not only urged but publicly *required* of men.
- Wine is forbidden, but so are all intoxicating drinks and other stimulants including tobacco.
- Modest dress is prescribed, including the type of clothing that should be worn, especially by women. A black burka, covering all but the eyes and hands, is specified.

Other restrictions include:

- Performing or listening to music
- Dancing
- Fortune telling
- Amulets
- Television programs (unless religious)
- Smoking

- Playing backgammon, chess, or cards
- Drawing human or animal figures
- Acting in a play or writing fiction (both are considered forms of lying)
- Dissecting cadavers (even in criminal investigations or for the purposes of medical research)
- Recorded music played over telephones on hold
- The sending of flowers to friends or relatives who are in the hospital
- Listening to music in praise of Muhammad
- Praying to God while visiting tombs (including the tomb of Muhammad)
- Celebrating the birthday of the Prophet
- Using ornamentation on or in mosques
- The driving of motor vehicles by women (which is permissible in every country except Wahhabi-dominated Saudi Arabia)

Disobeying any such requirements can be punished by flogging or worse.

In the 1970s, with the help of funding from petroleum exports and other factors, Saudi charities started funding Wahhabi schools (madrassas) and mosques across the globe, and the movement underwent explosive growth. The US State Department has estimated that over the past four decades, Riyadh (the capital of Saudi Arabia) has invested more than $10 billion dollars in charitable foundations in an attempt to replace mainstream Sunni Islam with the harsh intolerance of its Wahhabism. European Union intelligence experts estimate that 15 to 20 percent of this has been diverted to Al-Qaeda and other violent jihadists.

The 9/11 attacks in 2001 on Saudi Arabia's so-called ally, the United States, that killed almost 3,000 people and caused at least $10 billion in property and infrastructure damage, were assumed by many (at least outside of Saudi Arabia) to be an expression of Wahhabism, since

Al-Qaeda leader Osama bin Laden and most of the 9/11 hijackers were Saudi nationals.

In July of 2013, Wahhabism was identified by the European

Parliament in Strasbourg as the main source of global terrorism.

Wahhabism Today: The use of violence advocated by modern ultra-Wahhabists such as Al Qaeda, ISIL, and Boko Haram have now given rise to cells of activists outside Saudi Arabia, ready to commit terrorist outrages like those recently seen in Beirut, Paris, Nice, Brussels, Lahore, and the United States.

Writer Lincoln Clapper draws a connection between Wahhabism, ISIS, and the Saudis.

> *Firstly, ISIS is effectively using social media campaigns to recruit new members from all over the globe.*
>
> *Secondly, the size of the group (estimates are around 30,000) is large enough to conclude that a small-scale counterinsurgency campaign would not be enough to suppress its progress across the region due to their massive territorial control over northern Syria and parts of Iraq.*
>
> *Thirdly, ISIS controls oil fields that are estimated to be making them $3 million per day on the black market, and the toppling of the Iraqi bank in Mosul gave them an inheritance of nearly $400 million in cash. The continued kidnapping of foreigners and reporters will serve as possible additional funding from European and Asian governments due to their willingness to negotiate with terrorist organizations. ISIS's financial resources, recruiting tactics, and*

*military strength are all imperative issues facing the
international community moving forward.*

He continues:

> *It is blatant that the state religion in Saudi Arabia
> has both directly and indirectly led to the formation
> of ISIS. The Wahhabi ideology taught, enforced,
> and supported in Saudi Arabia is essentially a
> mirror image of the religious establishment ISIS is
> implementing in its attempt to form an Islamic state,
> with both the House of Shaykh and Al-Baghdadi
> adhering to the same teachings and theology of
> Wahhabism. While the conduct of Wahhabism in
> Saudi Arabia is not at the level of brutality that
> ISIS displays by leaving beheaded bodies mounted
> in the streets, enslaving women and girls of different
> religions, or massacring towns and villages at point-
> blank range, the fundamental ideas behind the
> importance of living by the Koran and ruling by the
> sword still pertain to both sides—this is evidenced
> by public opinion polls and support for the groups
> across internet platforms.*

> *As long as the Wahhabi ideology prevails as the
> religious authority in Saudi Arabia, the potential
> will always remain for additional Sunni groups
> to emerge with the same pious philosophies and
> inclinations as ISIS. The House of Shaykh and the
> House of Saud have deep, intertwined family ties
> with each other, as members of both houses have
> married one another over the last two centuries.
> The House of Saud will most likely never allow the
> House of Shaykh to lose its religious authority in the
> Kingdom because of the need for the House of Shaykh*

to legitimize the power the royal family possess. If the Saudi Arabian establishment is continually supported and backed by the West, their existence will be incompatible with countering Islamic radicalism. Moving forward, expect to see any rise of religious fanaticism inside the Kingdom suppressed while extremist groups outside of the Kingdom's grasp, particularly in neighboring countries, continue to emulate the Wahhabi doctrine that Saudi Arabia has lived under since its founding.

The Jakarta Summit: **A Hopeful Sign!**

Not enough publicity has been given to the Jakarta Summit, a meeting of Muslim leaders from around the world in Jakarta, Indonesia that began on May 9, 2016. More than 300 moderate religious leaders from 33 countries attended the two-day conference which was hosted by the Indonesian Muslim organization Nahdlatul Ulama ("Awakening of Scholars"), which claims 50 million members worldwide. They met to address the religious aspects of extremism and terrorism. A. Mustofa Bisri, the spiritual leader of Nahdlatul Ulama, addressed the International summit, saying:

> *According to the Sunni view of Islam, every aspect and expression of religion should be imbued with love and compassion, and foster the perfection of human nature.*

Both the President and the Vice President of Indonesia attended the summit. Vice President Jusuf Kalla of Indonesia denounced what he called radical youths' misinterpretation of the idea of jihad, saying that such extremists mistakenly view violence and terrorism as a "shortcut" to heaven.

> *That's why the role of Islamic clerics is needed to do more to correct the misinterpretation. . . . We gather here today for that purpose, to produce the solution to curb radicalism in the form of terrorism, wars and conflicts.*

Even though Indonesia has the largest Muslim population in the world (190 million), it has coexisted with Buddhists, Christians, and Hindus. Its society has thus developed a liberal brand of Islam. The leadership of the Nahdlatul Ulama (**NU**) believes this approach to Islam (called ***Islam Nusantara*** or *"Islam of the Archipelago"*) can be a powerful force against the radicalization of Islam.

NU has implemented a program among young Indonesians who volunteer their services as "Cyber Warriors" in order to counter the radical Islam's content on social media. However, this program is "minuscule" compared to the radical Muslims' network. The NU's youth wing held a three-day conference releasing the film *The Divine Grace of East Indies Islam* (***Rahmat Islam Misantara***). The film explores Islam's arrival in Indonesia and its evolution. It includes interviews with Indonesian Islamic Scholars. It has been translated into English and Arabic and placed online for international attention and distribution.

The film includes scenes in which radical Islam's interpretation of the Koran and hadith are shown as factually incorrect and even perverse. The film also calls attention to radical Islam's theology, rooted in the fundamentalist <u>**Wahhabi**</u> movement **(see section on "Wahhabism")** which is based on medieval Islamic jurisprudence, where slavery and the execution of prisoners were the norm. The filmmakers propose that Islamic law needs to be updated to the twenty-first century.

<u>**World Leaders:**</u> Several world leaders have called on Islamic leaders to come forward and take the lead in this ideological battle against the violence perpetrated by this offshoot of Islam. Nico Prucha, Research

Fellow at London's King's College, who analyzes radical Islam's Arab-Language online propaganda, states:

> *I see the counter-narrative as the only way that Western governments can deal with the ISIS propaganda, but there's no strategy right now. . . .*

The General Secretary of the NU Supreme Council added:

> *We are directly challenging the idea of ISIS, which wants Islam to be uniform, meaning that if there is any other idea of Islam that is not following their ideas, those people are infidels who must be killed . . . we will show that is not the case with Islam.*

One other problem that was identified at the Jakarta Summit was that non-Arab countries like Indonesia have **less** influence in the practice of Islam. Azyumardi Azra, an Islamic scholar and former Rector of the State Islamic University in Jakarta, addresses the problem by stating:

> *The problem with Middle East Islam is they have what I call religious racism. . . . They feel that only the Arabs are real Muslims and the others are not.*

JAKARTA DECLARATION

At the end of the Summit, the attendees published a *"Jakarta Declaration"* calling for an international coalition of religious groups and governments to dismantle the religious backing of extremism and terrorism. The Declaration—which, at the time of this writing, has not yet become official—is set to be submitted to the President, Vice President, and the Coordinating Political, Legal, and Security Ministry as well as foreign embassies in Indonesia soon.

According to the Declaration, the misinterpretation itself is the cause of the prolonged conflict in the Middle East, where some governments use religious teachings as the basis for their political legitimacy, which has given rise to religious extremism.

The economic and political injustice that has brought poverty to some Islamic countries has been used by extremist groups as one of their reasons for unleashing their terror, the declaration states, which has led to a misguided concept of jihad executed by these groups.

According to the Islam Nusantara perspective, Islamic teachings did not call for its believers to conquer the world but instead for them to keep strengthening their faith to realize Islam as a "Blessing for the Universe" (***Rahmatan lil alamin***).

The **Declaration** also urges the Indonesian government to play a constructive role as a mediator to find solutions for the multifaceted conflicts in the Middle East. In addition, the Islam Nusantara would assist Middle Eastern countries in building mechanisms to connect the concepts of Islam and nationalism if their governments were open and willing to build alternative bases for their political legitimacy.

Islam Nusantara Secretary-General Helmi Faisal Zaini said the countries that took part in the summit were all surprised to learn that Islam in Indonesia could be highly tolerant of local culture, for example, promoting the ancient Buddhist temple complex of Borobudur in Indonesia as a historical site.

Meanwhile, Fazal Ghani Kakar, the founder of Afghanistan's Islam Nusantara, said Islam Nusantara provided the best solution for conflicts not only in Afghanistan but in the entire Muslim world, since the paradigm was neither too liberal nor too extreme. The paradigm could even be adopted in non-Muslim conflict areas. NU promoted five general principles of moderation, tolerance, justice, balance, and participation that could bring people together and guard a country's unity. Kakar concludes:

> *"It's the best solution to make everybody understand that moderation is the way for a better life and humanity in general."*

The next summit will be arranged by Indonesia's NU and will probably be held in another country in the hopes that other recognized scholars or authorities in the religious hierarchy of religious studies (***ulemas***) will join the summit, even though the details of the next summit are not yet settled.

In his evaluation of the Summit, Dr. KH Said Aquil Siradj, Chairman of NU, states:

> *"The conclusion of our two-day meeting is the core of jihad, namely to promote peace and do good deeds."*

(1) "Twelver Shia Muslims" believe that the Twelve Imams are the spiritual and political successors to the prophet Muhammad. According to the theology of Twelvers, the Twelve Imams are exemplary human individuals who not only rule over the community in justice but also are able to keep and interpret sharia and the esoteric meaning of the Koran. The words and deeds (Sunnah) of Muhammad and the Imams are a guide and model for the community to follow; as a result, Muhammad and the Imams must be free from error and sin, known as Ismah or infallibility, and must be chosen by divine decree through Muhammad.

(2) Koran, Translated by M.H. Shakir (1999 Edition)

(3) The Decline of Eastern Christianity Under Islam; Bat Ye'or, pages 38, 40

(4) Salman Rushdie, NY Times, 11/02/01

(5) Suzerainty: A situation in which a powerful state or region controls the foreign policy and international relations of another state or region.

CHAPTER 9

THE FIVE PILLARS OF ISLAM

Islam is based on **five Pillars**. These Pillars refer to the five fundamental ritual duties which should be performed by every believer.

First Pillar: SHAHADAH

Shahadah is Arabic for "testify" or "announce." It is the confession of faith, similar to the practice of Christians to confess their faith by repeating one of the ancient creeds of the church or one of the more modern statements of faith. It literally means, *"I testify that there is no God except Allah, and I testify that Muhammad is his Messenger."* The believer is testifying to the unity of God and His creation as well as the legitimacy of Muhammad as His prophet. Non-Muslims who repeat the Shahadah three times of their own free will, in front of witnesses with honorable intent, is affirming their conversion to Islam, a step that can never be revoked.

Second Pillar: SALAH

Salah (or Salat) means "prayer." The prayers must be repeated five times a day, preferably with other Muslim believers. However, the prayers can be performed anywhere. No ground is "holy." Believers are called to prayer from the Minaret *(1)*. The times of prayer vary according to geography and the sun. The usual times are early morning or sunrise, early afternoon, late afternoon, early evening, and late evening. The believer is expected to attend the mosque for prayers, but it is not a requirement.

All males are expected to attend mosque on Fridays. At the mosque, all those in prayer align themselves in rows facing Mecca. Women either pray at home, in a separate room of the mosque, or separated from men by means of some kind of screen in the main hall of the mosque.

In order for prayer to be valid, cleanliness of clothing and location is necessary. The person praying should also undergo a ritual of purification. This involves washing *(2)*. Each sect of the Muslim religion has different requirements regarding what to wash and how.

Third Pillar: ZAKAH

Zakah, translated literally, means "sweeting" in Arabic or "to be pure; just." Another duty of Muslims is to share their earthly possessions with fellow believers who are less well-off or impoverished. The amount given is a legally determined tax of an exactly defined percentage of one's assets (2½ percent). Every healthy and free Muslim who has come of age must pay this tax. It shows their gratitude to Allah for the opportunity to live in prosperity. Through this tax, affluent Muslims are obligated to assume social responsibility; it cleanses the donor from greed. The tax is collected by the "state" if it is a Muslim state. If not a Muslim state, it is collected by the religious leader of the mosque. There are also voluntary alms or offerings wherein the donor determines the amount to be given.

Fourth Pillar: SAWM

Sawn means "fasting." During the thirty days of Ramadan, the ninth month of the Islamic Lunar Calendar, all healthy Muslims who are of age are obligated to participate in ritual fasting. Fasting begins at sunrise and lasts until sundown. Eating and drinking are not permitted, neither are such "hedonistic" pleasures such as tobacco, sexual activity, evil thoughts, or evil deeds (lying, cursing, arguing). It is customary to eat a light meal before dawn. After sundown, eating, drinking, and sex may resume. The aged, sick, menstruating women, and children are exempt from the duty of the fast.

The "Breaking of the Fast" at the end of Ramadan is celebrated with a feast, *(3)* which usually lasts three days.

Fifth Pillar: THE HAJJ

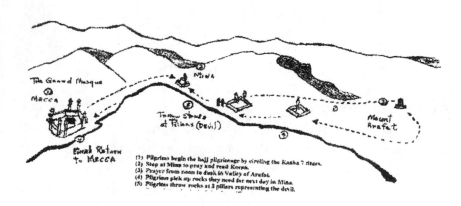

(1) Pilgrims begin the hajj pilgrimage by circling the Kaaba 7 times.
(2) Stop at Mina to pray and read Koran.
(3) Prayer from noon to dusk in Valley of Arafat.
(4) Pilgrims pick up rocks they need for next day in Mina.
(5) Pilgrims throw rocks at 3 pillars representing the devil.

The Hajj is the Islamic pilgrimage to Mecca. It takes place during the last month of the Islamic year. The hajj is commanded in the Koran - *"... pilgrimage to the House is incumbent upon men for the sake of Allah, everyone who is able to undertake the journey to it for mankind"* (4) - and its rites were supposedly established by Muhammad. The pilgrimage to Mecca was one of the last public acts of worship performed by Muhammad before his death. The hajj, to some extent, commemorates the stories of Abraham, Hagar and Ishmael and it has been assigned various other meanings throughout the centuries. The pilgrimage of today is not the same as the one Muhammad took over a thousand years ago. Certain procedures and rites have been added over the centuries by Islamic religious leaders.

Exceptions are made for those who are physically or financially unable to fulfill this obligation and one is actually commanded not to make the hajj if to do so would cause hardship for his or her family. However, those unable to go themselves may fulfill their obligation by sending someone in their place.

The hajj takes place during the final month (12th) of the Islamic Calendar *(5)* between the 8th and the 13th day of the month.

Day One: *(Eighth Day of the Month)* **Purification *(6)***

Upon arrival in Saudi Arabia, pilgrims set out from Mecca to the sprawling tent-city of Mina, whether by foot along pilgrim paths, or by buses and cars. It is a 6 mile journey. The pilgrims will spend the day in Mina to enter into a state of holiness or purity (ihram). Men are required to wear two white seamless sheets, with no knots or stitched items. Footwear allows only the ankle and back of the foot to be exposed, and no perfume must be used on the body. The common dress serves to contribute to a sense of equality and unity by removing visual indicators of class, wealth and culture. Cutting nails, shaving and sexual relations are all forbidden. Women are forbidden to wear the Burqa as they must have their faces uncovered. There is no gender segregation during hajj, to remind pilgrims that men and women will be standing side by side on the Day of Judgment – Allah's final assessment of humanity.

Pilgrims enter the Grand Mosque *(7)* and walk seven times counter-clockwise around (tawaf, or circumambulation) the Kaaba, the central cubical shaped building while reciting a prayer (talbiyah), then kisses or touches the Black Stone *(8)*. If crowds prevent this, a pilgrim may point to the stone. Eating is not permitted but the drinking of water is allowed, because of the risk of dehydration due to the often high humidity in Mecca. Men are encouraged to perform the first three circuits at a hurried pace. Afterwards, the pilgrims drink from the Zamzam (holy) Well – made available in coolers throughout the Mosque. The pilgrim then prays twice at the Station of Abraham.

Following the circumambulation *(9)* of the Kaaba, the pilgrim walks or runs seven times between the hills of Safa and Marwah *(10)*. The area is now entirely enclosed by the mosque and can be accessed via air-conditioned tunnels. Pilgrims are advised to walk the circuit, but two green pillars mark a short section of the path where they are allowed to run.

Day Two: *(Ninth Day of the Month)*

Pilgrims travel from Mina to the Plain of Arafat. The *"Day of Arafat"* is considered one of the most important days, not just of the Hajj but of the Islamic calendar. Before noon, pilgrims arrive at **Mount Arafat**, also known as Mercy Mount, an area of barren land about twenty kilometers east of Mecca, where they repent of their sins. This lasts until sunset and is known as "standing before God."

A pilgrim's Hajj is considered invalid if they do not spend the afternoon on Arafat. The Mount is the scene of the Prophet Muhammad's final sermon, and after making the 8 mile journey from Mina, pilgrims spend the day in reverent prayer. Elsewhere in the world, many Muslims choose to fast on this day.

After sunset, it is time to move again, this time to **Muzdalifah**—a 5 mile trip—where they spend the night under the stars. Many will also begin collecting pebbles for tomorrow's rites before departing again just before sunrise.

Day Three: *(Tenth Day of the Month)*

Day three is probably the longest day of the pilgrimage and the most dangerous. Pilgrims start the day in Muzdalifah and begin heading back to **Mina** before dawn. Once in Mina, they perform the throwing of the first of seven pebbles at the largest of three columns *(11)*. This act is the symbolic stoning of the devil based on historic tradition. God told Abraham to sacrifice his son (Ishmael) as proof of his faith. It is believed that at this spot in Mina, the devil appeared and tried to dissuade Abraham from heeding the command. Abraham responded by throwing stones to scare him off.

Millions of pilgrims converge at the **Jamarat Bridge**, which houses the three columns representing the devil in order to re-enact the story of Abraham rejecting Satan's temptation. This rite is performed ten times during the four days. For safety reasons, the pillars were replaced by long walls in 2004 with basins to collect the pebbles. The purpose of the bridge is to enable pilgrims to throw stones at the three pillars, either from ground level or from the bridge. After the casting of stones, pilgrims then must perform the Festival of the Sacrifice.

The Festival of the Sacrifice *(12)*, the second most important Muslim holiday, is also called the *"Sacrifice Feast"* and is celebrated by all Muslims around the world each year. It remembers and honors the willingness of Abraham to sacrifice his son (Ishmael), as an act of submission to Allah's command. Allah then intervened through his angel Gabriel and informed him that his sacrifice had already been accepted.

During the modern Festival of the Sacrifice, the meat from the sacrificed animal is supposed to be divided into three parts. The family retains one-third of the share; another third is given to relatives, friends, and neighbors; the remaining third is given to the poor and needy.

Among the most important objects a pilgrim will use on hajj are a simple pair of scissors and a razor. An obligatory ritual is the cutting or shaving of the hair, which occurs twice during hajj. The Saudi Arabian government provides licensed barbers with a new razor blade for each male pilgrim while women snip only a lock of hair. This act of devotion symbolizes the shedding of worldly attachments.

Many will then proceed to Mecca, circling the Kaaba seven times and then walking seven times between the hills of Safa and Marwa. When all is finally done, they return to their campsite in Mina.

Days Eleven through Thirteen

With the hardest part behind them, pilgrims will then spend the next two or three days in Mina.

On each day, they will again symbolically stone the devil—this time throwing seven pebbles at each of the three pillars. When their time in Mina is finished, the pilgrims return to Mecca to perform the final circulation of the Kaaba to "bid farewell"*(13)*. Before heading home, many also go to **Medina**, the second holiest city in Islam, where the Prophet Muhammad is buried along with his closest companions. Visiting Medina, however, is not a mandatory part of Hajj.

(1) **Minaret is the tower at the mosque to call Muslims to prayer.**
(2) **Abulation - ritual of purification**
(3) **id al-fitr is the feast at the end of Ramadan**
(4) **Koran 3:97**
(5) **Dhul al-Hijjah - "12 month of Islamic Calendar"**
(6) **Ihram - "purity" or "holiness"**
(7) **Masjid al-Haran - "The Grand Mosque of Mecca"**
(8) **Al-Hajar al-Aswad - "The Black Stone"**
(9) **Tawaf – "The circumambulation of the Ka'ba"**
(10) **Sa'ay – "The walk or run seven times between the two hills"**
(11) **Jamarat al- Aqabah – "Stoning of Satan"**
(12) **Eid al-Adha - "The Feast of the Sacrifice"**
(13) **Tawaf al-Wide - "to bid farewell"**

Muslim pilgrims perform a symbolic stoning of the devil as they thrown pebbles at a pillar on the middle of the third day of the hajj in Mina, audi Arabia. On each of the following two days, they must hit each of the three Pillars with seven pebbles, going in order from east to west. Thus at least 49 pebbles are needed for the ritual- more if some pebbles miss their mark. After the stoning is completed, every pilgrim must cut or shave their hair.

CHAPTER 10

RAMADAN

In Arabic, *Ramadan* means "scorching heat" or "dryness." Ramadan occurs in the ninth month of the Islamic lunar calendar. Before Muhammad and Islam, Arabs regarded Ramadan as a holy month. During this month, war and hunting were prohibited. Travel and the movement of goods across the desert were safe from attack.

Islamic tradition believes that Muhammad received his first revelation from Allah during Ramadan. Until Muhammad's break with the Jews of Medina, the fast was from <u>dusk</u> to <u>dawn</u>. But after his disagreement and break with the Jews, he changed it to the opposite, **dawn** to **dusk**.

The Koran, 2:185 states:

> *The month of Ramadan is that in which was revealed the Koran; a guidance for mankind, and clear proofs of the guidance, and the criterion (of right and wrong). And whosoever of you is present, let him fast the month, and whosoever of you is sick or on a journey, a number of other days. Allah desires for you ease; He desires not hardship for you; and that you should complete the period, and that you should magnify Allah for having guided you, and that perhaps you may be thankful.*

Muslim scholars believe that while the Koran was revealed over a period of twenty-three years, the *"Night of Power"* *(1)* is considered the night in which the first revelations of Islam occurred and the prophethood of Muhammed began. This night is in celebration of the arrival of the Koran.

When exactly did the Night of Power occur? This is often a point of debate among Muslim scholars. Some scholars say that this night is hidden. Some say it occurs on either the first, seventh, or nineteenth night of Ramadan. However, there is strong evidence that the true night occurs during the last ten days of Ramadan, specifically on one of the odd-numbered nights.

According to the Koran, fasting was also obligatory for prior nations and is a way to attain fear of God. *(2)* Allah proclaimed to Muhammad that fasting for His sake was not a new innovation in monotheism but rather an obligation practiced by those truly devoted to the oneness of God. The pagans of Mecca also fasted but only on the tenth day of the first month of the lunar calendar to extinguish the guilt of their sins and to avoid droughts.

Islam requires a rigorous fast *(3)* during this month for all healthy adult Muslims. This fast requires total abstention from food, smoking, drink, and sex from dawn to sunset during every day of the month of Ramadan. The **Fourth Pillar** of Islam is the obligation of fasting, which Ramadan fulfills. As previously mentioned, the aged, sick, menstruating women, and children are exempt from fasting.

The exact time of the beginning of Ramadan is never announced ahead of time. It begins when a specific holy man in Mecca sees the first break of day of the New Moon. The fast is regarded as a moral and religious action, especially meritorious. Muslims are urged to increase their service to Allah during this month. Islam designates two purposes for fasting:

1. Self-discipline
2. To feel sympathy for the hungry of the world

Ramadan is a time of spiritual reflection, improvement, and increased devotion and worship. Muslims are expected to put more effort into following the teachings of Islam. The fast begins at dawn and ends at sunset. The act of fasting is said to redirect the heart away from worldly activities, its purpose being to cleanse the soul by freeing it from harmful impurities. Ramadan also teaches self-discipline, self-control, sacrifice, and empathy for those who are less fortunate, thus encouraging actions of generosity and compulsory charity. It becomes compulsory for Muslims to start fasting when they reach puberty, so long as they are healthy, sane, and have no disabilities or illnesses. Many children endeavor to complete as many fasts as possible as practice for later life.

Exemptions to fasting are travel, menstruation, severe illness, pregnancy, and breastfeeding. However, many Muslims with medical conditions insist on fasting to satisfy their spiritual needs, although it is not recommended by the hadith. Those unable to fast still must make up the days missed later.

The qualities the Muslim is supposed to cultivate through fasting are: patience, forbearance, perseverance, and steadfastness in suffering and deprivation. Food and sex are considered to be two of man's weaknesses in regards to morality and righteousness. Therefore, man should seek to resist the temptations of these two "vices" through fasting. The Muslim sees every day in Ramadan as a new trial, and, if successful until sunset, the day is ended with a celebration of food and joy. Fasting then begins again at the next sunrise.

Fasting also is meant to empathize with the hungry and deprived of the world. The Muslim is reminded by the fast to sympathize with the deprived everywhere. Islam encourages voluntarily feeding the poor on every day of Ramadan. It is customary to eat a light meal *(4)* before dawn. Then, after sunset, a prayer is recited. *(5)*

Muslims continue to work during Ramadan. The prophet Muhammed said that it is important to keep a balance between worship and work. Observance of Ramadan may (or may not) impact someone's performance at work. Employees are expected to inform their employer if they are fasting.

'Id al Filr (*Feast of Breaking the Fast*) This feast marks the end of the fast. It occurs on the first day of the next month after Ramadan (*Shawwal*) **(6)** and lasts for three days. It is a joyful feast, giving thanks to Allah for helping faithful observers through their trials of abstinence. After a prayer, fresh clothes are put on; friends and acquaintances are visited; the cemetery is visited to pay respects to deceased relatives; gifts are exchanged; old grudges are dismissed. Giving alms to the poor is also part of the celebration.

(1) **Laylatul Qadr**
(2) **Tagwa**
(3) **Siyam**
(4) **Sahur**
(5) **Attarawih**
(6) **Tenth** month on Islamic calendar

Dates for the beginning of <u>RAMADAN</u>

Gregorian Calendar	*Lunar (Hijri) Calendar*
June 6, 2016	1437
May 27, 2017	1438
May 16, 2018	1439
May 6, 2019	1440
April 24, 2020	1441
April 13, 2021	1442
April 2, 2022	1443
March 23, 2023	1444
March 11, 2024	1445
March 1, 2025	1446

CHAPTER 11

THE EARLY CHRISTIAN FATHERS' REACTIONS TO ISLAM

I have chosen to let the early Christian Church Fathers' writings speak for themselves regarding how they reflected on the Islamic religion. Most of the following quotations are from the Eastern Orthodox branch of the Christian Church because they were the first to encounter threats, expansion, and persecution by Muslims. Writer Thomas King, in one of his articles on Shoebat.com (Rescue Christians.org), January 16, 2016, quotes the writings of the early Church Fathers in reaction to the Islamic religion.

St. John of Damascus (circa AD 645/676–749)

> *And there is also the up until now strong and people-deceiving superstition of the Ishmaelites, being the forerunner of Antichrist. And it is born from Ishmael, who was born from Hagar to Abraham, from which they are called Hagarenes and Ishmaelites. And they call them Saracens, as from (those empty of Sarah), because of what was said by Hagar to the angel: 'Sarah has sent me away empty.' So then, these were idolaters and reverenced the morning star and*

Aphrodite, who they indeed named Khabar in their own language, which means great. Therefore, until the time of Heraclius, they were plainly idolaters. From that time and until now came up among them a false prophet called Mamed (1), who, having encountered the Old and New Testament, as it seems, having conversed with an Arian monk, he put together his own heresy. And under the pretext of seeming pious, attracting (?) people, he reported that a book was sent down to him from heaven by God. Therefore, some of the compositions written by him in a book, worthy of laughter, which he handed down to them as an object of reverence.

He says there is one God, the Maker of all things, neither having been begotten nor having begotten. He says Christ is the Word of God and His Spirit, only a creation and servant, and that he was born without seed from Mary the sister of Moses and Aaron. For he says the Word of God and the Spirit went into Mary and she bore Jesus who was a prophet and servant of God. And that the Jews, acting against the law, wanted to crucify him and having seized (him), they crucified his shadow. For Christ himself, they say, was not crucified nor did he die, for God took him to himself into heaven because he loved him. . . .

Mamed speaks again (in) the writing of The Table. And he says that Christ asked God for a table, and he gave it to him. For God, he says, said to him that "I have given to you and to yours an incorruptible table.

> *Again, the writing of The Cow, and some other*
> *foolish sayings worthy of laughter, I think I should*
> *skip because of their number. He legislated that*
> *they be circumcised, including the women, and*
> *also commanded not to keep the Sabbath, nor to be*
> *baptized, and to eat some of the things forbidden in*
> *the Law, and to avoid (some of) those it permitted.*
> *And he entirely forbade the drinking of wine.*

Abo, The Perfumer of Baghdad, Martyr and Saint (? –A.D 786)

> *You are quite right saying that I am a Saracen by*
> *blood, born into that race on both father's and*
> *mother's side. I was educated in the religion of*
> *Muhammad, and lived according to it as long as*
> *I remained in ignorance. But when the Almighty*
> *had mercy on me and selected me from among my*
> *brothers and relatives and saved me through His Son*
> *Jesus Christ my God, and granted me a more perfect*
> *understanding, then I quitted my former faith, as*
> *being a manmade creed based on fables thought up*
> *by human subtlety and invention. So now I cling to*
> *the true faith of the Holy Trinity, Father, Son and*
> *Holy Ghost, as revealed to us by Jesus Christ. In*
> *that faith I have been baptized and now worship,*
> *for this is the True God, and now I am a Christian*
> *unwavering in my conviction. I thank and bless Thee,*
> *O Holy Trinity, that Thou hast made me worthy to*
> *take part in the feats of Thy holy martyrs!*

> *—Abo, The Perfumer of Baghdad*

Abo, the perfumer of Baghdad, ended his life as a martyr, refusing to recant his faith in Christ.

—Thomas King

St. Sophronius, Patriarch of Jerusalem (AD 560–638)

St. Sophronius was not only Patriarch of Jerusalem but revered by Orthodox and Latins (Roman Catholics) alike. He died brokenhearted over the fall of Jerusalem to the Muslims under Abu Bakr, successor of Muhammad. Before the takeover of Jerusalem by Islamic forces, he said the following in a Christmas Sermon, around either AD 637 or 638, regarding the Arab Islamic invasion of Jerusalem.

—Thomas King

But the present circumstances are forcing me to think differently about our way of life, for why are [so many] wars being fought among us? Why do barbarian raids abound? Why are the troops of the Saracens attacking us? Why has there been so much destruction and plunder? Why are there incessant outpourings of human blood? Why are the birds of the sky devouring human bodies? Why have churches been pulled down? Why is the cross mocked? Why is Christ, who is the dispenser of all good things and the provider of this joyousness of ours, blasphemed by pagan mouths so that he justly cries out to us: "Because of you my name is blasphemed among the pagans," and this is the worst of all the terrible things that are happening to us. That is why the vengeful and God-hating Saracens, the abomination of desolation clearly foretold to us by the prophets, overrun the places which are not allowed to them, plunder cities, devastate fields, burn down villages, set on fire the holy churches, overturn the sacred monasteries, oppose the Byzantine armies arrayed against them, and in fighting raise up the trophies [of war] and add victory to victory. Moreover, they are raised up more and more against us and increase their blasphemy of Christ and the church, and utter wicked blasphemies against God. Those God- fighters boast of prevailing over all, assiduously and unrestrainably imitating their leader, who is the devil, and emulating his vanity because of which he has been expelled from heaven and been assigned to the gloomy shades.

We, however, because of our innumerable sins and serious misdemeanors, are unable to see these things, and are prevented from entering Bethlehem by way of the road. Unwillingly, indeed, contrary to our wishes, we are required to stay at home, not bound closely by bodily bonds, but bound by fear of the Saracens. . . . At once that of the Philistines, so now the army of the godless Saracens has captured the divine Bethlehem and bars our passage there, threatening slaughter and destruction if we leave this holy city and dare to approach our beloved and sacred Bethlehem. . . . If we were to live as is dear and pleasing to God, we would rejoice over the fall of the Saracen enemy and observe their near ruin and witness their final demise. For their blood-loving blade will enter their hearts, their bow will be broken and their arrows will be fixed in them . . . the godless Saracens entered the holy city of Christ our Lord, Jerusalem, with the permission of God and in punishment for our negligence, which is considerable, and immediately proceeded in haste to the place which is called the Capitol. They took with them men, some by force, others by their own will, in order to clean that place and to build that cursed thing, intended for their prayer and which they call a mosque.

—St. Sophronius

St. Peter Mavimenus (8ᵗʰ Century A.D.)

"Whoever does not embrace the Catholic Christian faith is lost, like your false prophet Muhammad".

His response as reported in the "Martyriologum Romanum" when he was asked to convert to Islam. He was martyred.

St. John Damascene (d. 749 A.D.)

There is also the superstition of the Ishmaelites which to this day prevails and keeps people in error, being a forerunner of the Antichrist...From that time to the present a false prophet names Mohmmed has appeared in their midst. This man, after having chanced upon the Old and New Testaments and likewise, it seems, having conversed with an Aria monk, devised his own heresy. Then, having insinuated himself into the good graces of the people by a show of seeming piety, he gave out that a certain book has been sent down from heaven. He has set down some ridiculous compositions in this book of his and he gave it to them as an object of veneration." **(1)**

Saints Habenitus, Jeremiah, Peter, Sabinian, and Walabonus (9ᵗʰ Century A.D.)

"We profess Christ to be truly God and your prophet to be a precursor of the Antichrist and other profane doctrines."

They were martyrs in Cordoba, Spain when asked to convert to Islam. (reported in the "Memoriale Sancorum").

Saints Aurelius, Felix, George, Liliosa, and Natalia (9ᵗʰ Century A.D.)

"any cult which denies the divinity of Christ, does not profess the existence of the Holy Trinity, refutes baptism, defames Christians, and derogates the priesthood, we consider to be damned."

(reported in the "Memoriale Sancorum")

St. Francis of Assisi (AD 1181–1226)

> *Those who believed in him were brutal men and desert wanderers, utterly ignorant of all divine teaching, through whose numbers Muhammad forced others to become his followers by the violence of his arms. Nor do divine pronouncements on the part of preceding prophets offer him any witness. On the contrary, he perverts almost all the testimonies of the Old and New Testaments by making them into fabrications of his own, as can be seen by anyone who examines his law. It was, therefore, a shrewd decision on his part to forbid his followers to read the Old and New Testaments, lest these books convict him of falsity. It is thus clear that those who place any faith in his words believe foolishly.*

> *—St. Francis of Assisi*

> *In August of 1219, Saint Francis of Assisi went to Egypt and confronted the Muslim caliph at Damietta along the banks of the Nile, which is that river in Egypt. Contrary to some revisionist*

accounts, he thoroughly supported the Fifth Crusade, five thousand of whose crusaders had been slain by Muslims just four days before, and he boldly urged the Muslims to accept Jesus Christ as their Lord and Savior. While it is true that he returned to Italy laden with some gifts from the intrigued, or bemused, caliph, he did so only after having been beaten, chained, and imprisoned.

—Thomas King

St. Thomas Aquinas (AD 1225–1274)

On the other hand, those who founded sects committed to erroneous doctrines proceeded in a way that is opposite to this. The point is clear in the case of Muhammad. He seduced the people by promises of carnal pleasure to which the concupiscence of the flesh goads us. His teaching also contained precepts that were in conformity with his promises, and he gave free rein to carnal pleasure. In all this, as is not unexpected, he was obeyed by carnal men. As for proofs of the truth of his doctrine, he brought forward only such as could be grasped by the natural ability of anyone with a very modest wisdom. Indeed, the truths that he taught he mingled with many fables and with doctrines of the greatest falsity. He did not bring forth any signs produced in a supernatural way, which alone fittingly gives witness to divine inspiration; for a visible action that can be only divine reveals an invisibly inspired teacher of truth. On the contrary, Muhammad said that he was sent in the power of his arms—which are signs not lacking even to robbers and tyrants. What is more, no wise men, men trained in things divine and human, believed in him from the beginning. Those who believed in him were brutal men and desert wanderers, utterly ignorant of all divine teaching, through whose numbers Muhammad forced others to become his followers by the violence of his arms. Nor do divine pronouncements on the part of preceding prophets offer him any witness. On the contrary, he perverts almost all the testimonies of the Old and New Testaments by making them into fabrications of his own, as can be seen by anyone who examines his law. It was, therefore, a shrewd decision on his part to forbid his followers to read the Old and New Testaments, lest these books convict him of falsity. It is thus clear that those who place any faith in his words believe foolishly.

—St. Thomas Aquinas

St. Gregory Palamas (AD 1296–1359)

In a debate at a Turkish nobleman's palace, St. Gregory Palamas stated:

It is true that Muhammad started from the east and came to the west, as the sun travels from east to west. Nevertheless he came with war, knives, pillaging, forced enslavement, murders, and acts that are not from the good God but instigated by the chief manslayer, the devil. Consider now, in times past, did not Alexander (the Great) prove victorious from the West to the East? There have also been many others, in many other times, who set out on military campaigns and dominated the world. Yet none of the peoples believed in their leaders as you revere Muhammad. Though Muhammad may employ violence and offer pleasures, he cannot secure the approval of the world. Albeit, the teaching of Christ, though it turns away from (worldly) pleasures, it has taken hold to the ends of the world, without violence, since it is opposed to it. This phenomenon is the victory that overcomes the world

—1 John 5:4

St. Juan de Ribera (d. 1611 A.D.)

"As we have seen, Muhammed had neither supernatural miracles nor natural motives of reason to persuade those of his sect. As he lacked in everything, he took to bestial and barbaric means, which is the force of arms. Thus he introduced and promulgated his message with robberies, murders, and blood-shedding, destroying those who did not want to receive it, and with the same means his ministers conserve this today, until God placates his anger and destroys this pestilence from the earth.

(Muhammad) can also be figured for the dragon in the same Apocalypse which says that the dragon swept up a third of the stars and hurled down a third to earth. Although this line is more appropriately understood concerning the Antichrist, Mohammed was his precursor – the prophet of Satan, father of the sons of haughtiness.

Even if all the things contained in his law were fables in philosophy and errors in theology, even for those who do not possess the light of reason, the very manners (Islam) teaches are from a school of vicious bestialities. (Muhammad) did not prove his new sect with any motive, having neither supernatural miracles nor natural reasons, but solely the force of arms, violence, fictions, lies, and carnal license. It remains an impious, blasphemous, vicious cult, an innovation of the devil, and the direct way into the fires of hell. It does not even merit the name of being called a religion." (2)

St. Alfonsus Liguori (d. 1787)

> *"The Mahometan paradise, however, is only fit for beasts; for filthy sensual pleasure is all the believer has to expect there." (3)*

The Protestant Reformers of the Sixteenth Century, Luther and Calvin

After the Turks in their homeland Turkmenistan became Muslims, most of them later left and exported Islam into Southern Russia and the Ukraine. Other Muslims later spread Islam throughout the whole of Northern India, Malaysia, the Western Philippines, and Indonesia. Others spread it from North Africa across the Sahara into West Africa, East Africa, and thereafter into Southern Africa. Its advance into Europe was stopped—temporarily—only in 1683 right outside the Walls of Vienna in Austria.

The Protestant Reformation also occurred in a time of conflict as Christian Europe was threatened by the Muslim Ottoman Empire. Both Martin Luther and John Calvin lived with the ongoing tension of a possible invasion of Europe by the Turkish armies. The Reformation period was bookended by two attempts to conquer the city of Vienna, in 1529 and 1683. This meant that there was a lot of fear and tension in the hearts of Christians towards Muslims. Luther and Calvin had similar reactions to this perceived Islamic threat, although Luther was more sympathetic to Islam than Calvin. Luther believed that Muslims and Christians worshiped the one

Creator and Eternal God, albeit Muslims worshiped
Him incorrectly.

—Thomas King

Luther

Luther wrote that the *"two regimes, that of the Pope and that of the Turks,*
are . . . antichrist." He noted that Christ warned about false prophets
coming from the desert (Matthew 24:24–26), and this certainly
included Muhammad. He also observed from 1 John 2:18–

22 and 4:1–3, *"Who is the liar? It is the man who denies that Jesus is the*
Christ. Such a man in the antichrist—he denies the Father and the Son";
and that the *"Mohammedans deny both the Fatherhood of God and the*
Deity of Christ—hence they are liars. They testify against the truth of God's
word."

Luther also believed that the Muslim Turks wanted *"to eradicate the*
Christians." In his final sermon, Luther preached that *"Muslims, Jews*
and some heathen worship the one eternal God, the wise and just Creator
of heaven and earth to whom all human beings owe obedience." Luther also
believed that Muslims were lost because they did not believe the Gospel.
In his treatise *War Against the Turks* (1529), he wrote, *"Muslims destroy*
true religion by denying Christ as God's Son and his sacrifice."

Calvin

Calvin, in a sermon on Deuteronomy 18:15, maintained that Muhammad
was one of "the two horns of antichrist." In his commentaries on Daniel
(7:7–18), Calvin put forward the theory that the Muslim Turks were the
little horn that sprang up from the beast. As the Turks had conquered
much of the old Roman Empire, much of the prophecies concerning
Rome could apply to the Muslim world. Islam was one of the two legs

of the later Roman Empire described in Daniel 2. Commenting on Daniel 11:37, Calvin wrote that Muhammad *"allowed to men the brutal liberty of chastising their wives and thus he corrupted that conjugal love and fidelity which binds the husband to the wife . . . Mohamet (1) allowed full scope to various lusts—by permitting a man to have a number of wives . . . Mohamet invented a new form of religion."*

Commenting on 2 Thessalonians 2:3–12, Calvin wrote that . . . *"the sect of Mohammad was like a raging overflow, which in its violence tore away about half of the church."* In his commentary on 1 John 2:18–23, Calvin states that the Turks *"have a mere idol in place of God."*

On 1 John 4:3–6: *"but every spirit that does not acknowledge Jesus, is not from God. This is the spirit of the antichrist . . . this is how we recognize the spirit of truth and the spirit of falsehood."* Calvin noted that *"Mohammad too asserts that he has drawn his dreams only from Heaven. . . . False spirits claim the Name of God."* The 1643 Westminster Assembly's **Larger Catechism** calls on Christians to . . . **"pray, that the** *kingdom of sin and Satan may be destroyed, that the Gospel propagated throughout the world. . . ."*

In **Directory for the Public Worship of God**, he instructs congregations to *"pray for the propagation of the Gospel and Kingdom of Christ to all nations, for the conversion of the Jews, the fullness of the gentiles, the fall of antichrist, and the deliverance of the distressed Churches abroad from the tyranny of the anti-Christian faction, and from the cruel oppression and blasphemies of the Turk."*

Commenting on Revelation 9:1–11, the **Dutch Dordt Bible** of 1637 suggests that Muhammad is "Apollyon" (Greek for the Hebrew word "Abaddon," which means destroyer), and the army of locusts and scorpions are the Arab and Saracen armies that wage jihad in Muhammad's name.

In his *Institutes of the Christian Religion*, (Book 2, Chapter 6:4), Calvin writes: *"So today the Turks, although they proclaim at the top of their lungs that the Creator of Heaven and earth is God, still, while repudiating Christ, substitute an idol in the place of the true God."*

John Calvin explained in *Sermons on Timothy and Titus*, in a sermon on 2 Timothy 1:3, *"The Turks at this day, can allege and say for themselves: 'We serve God from our ancestors!'... It is a good while ago since Mahomet gave them the cup of his devilish dreams to drink, and they got drunk with them. It is about a thousand years since those cursed hellhounds were made drunk with their follies. ... Let us be wise and discreet! ... For otherwise, we shall be like the Turks and Heathen!"*

Calvin pointed out that the reign of the antichrist will be destroyed by the Word of God (2 Thessalonians 2:8).

> *Paul does not think that Christ will accomplish this in a single moment. . . . Christ will scatter the darkness in which antichrist will reign, by the rays which He will emit before His coming—just as the sun, before becoming visible to us, chases away the darkness of the night with its bright light. This victory of the Word will therefore be seen in the World. For "the Breath (or Spirit) of His Mouth" means simply His Word . . . as in Isaiah 11:4, the passage to which Paul appears to be alluding . . . It is a notable commendation of true and sound doctrine that it is represented as being sufficient to put an end to all ungodliness, and as destined at all times to be victorious over all devices of Satan. It is also a commendation when . . . a little further on . . . the preaching of this doctrine, is referred to as Christ's 'coming' to us.*
>
> *—John Calvin, Commentary on Second Thessalonians*

Calvin believed that Muslims, Pagans, and Jews were cut off from the church because they resisted the Gospel. Calvin wrote in his **Sermons on Deuteronomy**, *"The Christian faith is impugned by the wicked which pretend not to come unto God and by the Turks, the Pagans, and Jews. They blaspheme with open mouth . . . they be utterly cut off from the Church— like rotten members. Their resisting of the Gospel and their striving to abolish the Christian Religion—is no great wonder to us. . . ."*

Calvin did agree that if a Turk (Muslim) gave a satisfactory confession in the church, he or she could be baptized (Institutes 4:16–24).

Thomas King offers this conclusion:

> *It is clear from the Holy Scripture and the Holy Fathers and Saints that Islam is indeed a threat to both the Christian Faith and to the Church as well as the world. May many professing Christians in the Orthodox Church as well as the other denominations, wake up and to use the words of the late Father Seraphim Rose, "Be Christians once again," and thus defend Christ our God and Divine Spouse. May Christians not only have a real appreciation of the dangers of Islam but also a compassion willing to bring Muslims to the Only Way, Truth and Life: our Lord Jesus Christ (John 14:6). Christ died for sinners of whom I am chief (1 Timothy 1:15). This knowledge is the source of our salvation and the salvation of the world, and hence we appeal as Christians with all compassion, for Muslims to turn to the true Jesus Christ of Scripture, Who is fully God and fully man, Who died for the sins of mankind, Who rose again from the dead, and Who is returning as Judge for the living and the dead to give unto man according to his works. May Orthodox and all other Christians*

be willing to face this evil religion by the horns and pull souls out from the miry pit that sinks into hell, even if it means we lose our lives for the sake of the Gospel of Christ. God bless. Glory be to the Father, and to the Son and to the Holy Spirit, both now and unto the ages upon ages, world without end. Amen.

(1) *"One Heresies", section "On the Heresy of the Ishmaelites (in the Fathers of the Church, Vol. 37. Translated by Catholic University of America, CUA Press (1958), pages 153-160*

(2) *"Catechism papa la Instruccion de los Nievos Convertidos de los Moros" (1599)*

(3) *"The History of Heresies and their Refutation" published by James Duffy, 1847*

CHAPTER 12

THE CRUSADES (1095–1291)

A Brief Overview

Today, we have several definitions for "war." There are those who believe that there should "Never be Wars" (pacifists); those who believe in only "Just Wars"; those who believe in "Preventative Wars"; those who believe in only "Defensive Wars"; and those who believe that "Wars are for subduing peoples and building empires."

Having lived during the time of six wars—and having personally experienced one war firsthand—I wholeheartedly agree with the Civil War soldier General William T. Sherman, who said, **"War is Hell!"**

Which definition of war best fits or describes the Crusades? Modern-day Muslims consider the Crusades to be unprovoked and unjust wars against their empire and religion, *"when a band of Christian savages invaded the peaceful lands of Islam."(1)* Or, *". . . the crusades are those aggressive wars of expansion fought by religious fanatics in order to evict Muslims from their homeland, and force conversions to Christianity."(2)*

We will look at the Crusades through the eyes of five contemporary scholars and examine their interpretation of the Crusades. *(3)*

What Happened in the Middle East? Over the course of four centuries, the Muslims (acting out of Islamic jihad) wiped out over 50 percent of all the Christians in the world and conquered over 60 percent of all Christian lands—**before** the Crusades began. Scholars today believe there were over two million Christians in the Middle East (the birthplace of Christianity) prior to the rise of Islam.

> *It was the Muslim armies which had spread Islam from Saudi Arabia across the whole of Christian North Africa into Spain and even France within the first century after the death of Muhammad. Muslim armies sacked and slaughtered their way across some of the greatest Christian cities in the world including Alexandria, Carthage, Antioch and Constantinople. These Muslim invaders destroyed over 3,200 Christian churches just in the first 100 years of Islam. (4)*

Today, there are estimates that there are less than 200,000 Christians in the Middle East and decreasing due to the War in Syria, the rise of ISIS, and the religious persecution, restrictions, and harassment of Christians in the other Muslim countries in Africa and in the Middle East and the Far East.

Calling for a Crusade: Pope Urban II issued the first call for a Crusade in AD 1095. He did this in a speech at the Council of Clermont in southern France and called on the knighthood of France to liberate the Christians of the East and the Holy City of Jerusalem. His reasons for a Crusade were:

- The Turks were severely persecuting the Christians in the Middle East, even murdering them.
- The Turks had taken over territory previously belonging to Christians, including Jerusalem and sites that were considered holy.

- Christ commanded it.

Since this Crusade or "Armed Pilgrimage" would be difficult and dangerous, Urban decreed that all past sins of those who shouldered the burden would be forgiven.

> *"The crusades were but a response to more than four centuries of conquests in which Muslims had already captured over two-thirds of the Christian world."(5)*

Dr. Riley-Smith points out that the goals of the Crusades were:

1. To rescue the Christians of the East (many thousands of Christians were either slaves or imprisoned and tortured by the Muslims)
2. The liberation of Jerusalem and other places made holy by Christ

> *"The Crusaders' conquest of Jerusalem, therefore, was not colonialism, but an act of restoration and an open declaration of one's love of God." (6)*

But the Crusades were not just "holy wars" waged by purely virtuous soldiers whose piety led them to acts of self-sacrificing bravery. Like **all** wars, the Crusades involved a mix of good and bad conduct and motivations. Greed, cruelty, and slaughter occurred on both sides. There was conquest and defeat and re-conquest during those years, which ultimately led to the rise of a new Islamic Empire that threatened Europe, only to be stopped at the gates of Vienna in 1683. *(7)*

AND THE CRUSADES BEGAN

The First Crusade (1096–1099): Four armies of Crusaders were formed in different regions of Western Europe. Prior to the departure of the main armies, a less-organized band of knights and commoners (known as the "People's Commoners") commanded by a preacher known as Peter the Hermit left for the Middle East. Peter's army went through the Byzantine Empire (Christian), leaving destruction in their wake. They crossed into Turkey, and, in the first major conflict between the Crusaders and the Muslim forces, Peter the Hermit's Crusaders were soundly defeated. Another group of Crusaders carried out a series of massacres of Jews in various towns of the Rhineland.

When the four main armies of Crusaders arrived in Constantinople, the Patriarch of Constantinople insisted their leaders swear an oath of loyalty to him and recognize his authority over any land regained from the Turks. They *did not* swear the oath of loyalty.

> 1097—The four main armies of Crusaders and their Byzantine allies captured Nicaea (Turkey).
>
> 1098—The Crusaders captured the Syrian city of Antioch.
>
> 1099—The Crusaders captured Jerusalem. (Despite their promise to the governor of protection, the Crusaders slaughtered hundreds of men, women, and children, Jews and Muslims alike, in their victorious entrance into the city.)

The Crusaders established four Crusader States: Jerusalem, Edessa, Antioch, and Tripoli.

The Second Crusade (1147–1149): Muslim forces recaptured Edessa in 1144, which prompted the Call for the Second Crusade.

> 1147—The Turks crushed the Crusaders' army at the site of the Crusaders' first great victory. The same year, the Crusaders army of 50,000 attacked Damascus, Syria and were defeated, ending the Second Crusade.

The Third Crusade (1189–1192): The Crusaders were forced to evacuate Cairo in 1169. Then in 1187, the Muslims defeated the Crusader army in Jerusalem. Outrage over these defeats is what prompted the Third Crusade.

> 1191—The Crusaders, led by Richard the Lionheart, defeated the Muslim forces in the battle of Arsuf, recapturing the city of Jaffa and re-establishing control over the region.

> 1192—Richard signed a peace treaty with sultan Saladin that re-established the Kingdom of Jerusalem, which ended the Third Crusade.

The Fourth Crusade (1198–1204): The Crusaders diverted from their primary mission in order to topple the Byzantine Emperor.

> 1204—The Crusaders declared war on Constantinople. The conquest and looting of Constantinople ended the Fourth Crusade.

OTHER CRUSADES

Albigensian Crusade (1208–1229): This Crusade aimed at rooting out heretical Christian sects primarily in Europe.

Baltic Crusades (1211–1225): These Crusades sought to subdue paganism in Transylvania.

The Children's Crusade (1212): There are at least three different accounts of the Children's Crusade. I have chosen to relate the "traditional" story of this Crusade. There was a boy who began preaching in either Germany or France, that he had been visited by Jesus. Jesus allegedly told him to lead a Crusade to "peacefully" convert the Muslims to Christianity. He gained a considerable following of

30,000 children through his preaching and by supposedly performing miracles. He led his followers south towards the Mediterranean Sea, in the belief that the sea would part on their arrival, allowing them to march to Jerusalem. Obviously, this did not happen. The children were subsequently tricked by two merchants who offered to provide free passage by boat to Jerusalem. Instead, the children were either taken to Tunisia and sold into slavery or died in a shipwreck during a storm. Some of the children never made it to the Mediterranean Sea, dying or giving up from starvation and exhaustion, betrayed by some of the adults who were part of their group.

The Fifth Crusade (1215–1221): The Crusaders attacked Egypt by land and by sea but were forced to surrender to a large, combined army of Muslims.

The Sixth Crusade (1229): Emperor Frederick II was able to achieve a peaceful transfer of Jerusalem to the Crusaders with the Muslim officials. The agreement, however, was short-lived. Ten years later, the peace treaty expired, and Muslims once again controlled Jerusalem.

The Seventh Crusade (1239–1241): The Crusaders again led an assault on Egypt and were again defeated.

The Last Crusade (1289–1291): In 1289, the Crusaders were once again defeated, and the Muslims recaptured Tripoli. The Muslims also recaptured Acre in 1291, ending two centuries of Crusades to the Holy Land.

After 1291, the Church (Rome) organized minor Crusades with limited goals, aimed at pushing Muslims out of conquered territory or conquering pagan regions. Support for such efforts disappeared in the sixteenth century with the rise of the Reformation and the decline of papal authority.

REV. THEODORE BOWERS

(1) Dr. Brian M. English
(2) Dr. Peter Hammond
(3) Dr. Bruce M. English; Dr. Bruce Frohnen; Dr. Peter Hammond; Dr. Thomas Madden; and Dr. Riley-Smith.
(4) Dr. Peter Hammond
(5) Dr. Thomas Madden
(6) Dr. Riley-Smith.
(7) Dr. Bruce Frohnen

CHAPTER 13

Islam Today

What we are seeing in our world today is the alarming rise of "Radical" Islam. It is a threat not only to those in the non-Muslim world but also to the Muslim world itself.

Evidence of conflict among Muslims dates back to the beginnings of the religion with the division of the Sunni and the Shia. But the causes for the rise of "Radical" Islam are many and complicated. To name a few:

- Poverty
- Lack of industrialization
- Muslims perceiving the threat of westernization
- Lack of natural resources (except for oil)
- The philosophy of their religion
- Their lifestyle
- Their educational system
- Their lack of democracy
- The basic Islamic understanding of God
- Their elevation of Muhammad to godlike status
- Religion as their political system (theocracy)

What we need to acknowledge is that Islam is **NOT** a "religion of peace." From the beginnings of Islam, Muhammad and the leaders who followed him waged wars against pagans, Christians, Jews, Zoroastrians, and atheists (infidels). The "enemies of Islam" were given the option of paying additional taxes, were forbidden to propagate their religion, and had to wear distinctive clothes to separate them from Muslims . . . or suffer death and slavery. Thousands of churches and synagogues were either destroyed or turned into mosques. Any peace agreements were always in terms of Islam's conditions and lasted only as long as the Islamic ruler decided it would last.

Muslim Population: According to Pew Research, the Muslim population growth rate:

> 2010. . . . 1.6 billion Muslims, or 23.4 % of the world population
>
> 2020. . . . 1.9 billion Muslims, or 24.9 % of the world population
>
> 2030. . . . 2.2 billion Muslims, or 26.4 % of the world population
>
> 2050. . . . 2.8 billion Muslims, or 29.7 % of the world population

According to Wikipedia, there are forty-nine countries in the world that have more than a 50 percent Muslim population.

It is estimated by Muslim researchers that <u>only</u> 10 to 15 percent of Muslims support jihad (Holy War). If they are correct, this means there are between 160 million and 240 million jihadists. Of course, a majority of Muslims are **not** Jihadist but want to live peaceably. But they are a <u>**silent**</u> majority that needs to speak out and voice their disapproval and rejection of Holy War.

Islamist Terrorist Attacks: The number of radical Islamist attacks continues to increase over the past thirty-three years.

1983 to 1989—9

1990 to 1999—31

2000 to 2002—60

2003 to 2005—64

2006 to 2009—25

2010 to 2014—103

2015 to 2010—118

2016 (Jan 1 to May 11)—28

(*Numbers taken from Wikipedia*)

Terrorists' attacks are not all against people of other religions but also against other Islamists who do not agree with the terrorists' particular belief system. There are several reasons for the increase in Islamic terrorism, but I would like to explore just two: social media and schools.

Social Media: Television and Internet are two sources utilized by jihadists to propagate their propaganda and to recruit members for jihad. I would like to share the words of some jihadists from the film ***Obsession, Radical Islam's War Against the West. (1)***

2001 Palestinian TV—Sheikh ibralim Madhi: *"We must educate our children on the love of jihad for the sake of Allah. And the love of fighting for the sake of Allah."*

2002 Palestinian TV—Ahmed Abdal Razek (Palestinian Cleric):

"Should we want honor? The only way to honor is jihad!"

<u>2003 Iraqi TV</u>—<u>Sheikh Dr. Bakr Al-Samarai</u>: *"The Americans and their president and the British and those that follow them and the Zionists, the spoiled offspring of the entity. . . . If Allah permits us, Oh Nation of Mohammad, even the stone will say, 'Oh Muslim, a Jew is hiding behind me, come and cut off his head.' And we shall cut off his head! By Allah, we shall cut it off! Oh Jews! . . . Jihad for the sake of Allah! . . . Victory for Allah. Allahu Akbar (God is great!)."*

<u>2003 Palestinian TV</u>—<u>Sheikh ibralim Mudeiris</u>: *"America is the foremost enemy of the Muslim nation, because it wages war against the Arab, Islamic nation."*

<u>2004 Iranian TV</u>—<u>Nagi Al-Shihabi</u>: (Newspaper Editor) *"The truth is that the US wants to eradicate our religious and Islamic identity."*

<u>2004 Iranian TV</u>—<u>Ayatollah Ahmad Jannati</u>: *"They have come to fight the people of Iraq. Basically, they have come to fight Islam. . . . All the Arab countries and the non-Arab countries will be their targets. They continue the line of swallowing the world. . . . Therefore, every Muslim and every honorable man who is not a Muslim must stand against the Americans, English, and Israelis and endanger their interests wherever they may be."*

<u>2004 Lebanon TV</u>—<u>Hassan Nasrallah</u>: (Hezbollah) *"The Americans must understand that they attack holy places, they attack all the Muslims of the world. . . ."*

<u>2004 Saudi Arabia TV</u>—<u>Sheikh Muhammad Al-Munajid</u>: *A British teenager tore out an elderly woman's heart after stabbing her and drank her blood. There are people (in the West) who are enthusiastic about drinking elderly peoples' blood."*

<u>2004 Iranian TV</u>—*"America is lurking for you, and will not give up until it destroys you completely soon because the world is not safe from the hunter. . . . The world without America!"*

2004 United Arab Emirates TV—Mamoun Al-Tamimi: (Political Commentator) *"They (The Americans) are beasts in human form."*

2005 Lebanon TV—Hasswen Nasrallah: (Hezbollah Sec. General) *"The most honorable death is by killing. And the most honorable killing and most glorious martyrdom is when a man is killed for the sake of Allah."*

2005 Lebanon TV—Anis Al-Naqqash: (Researcher) *"The US is the enemy of Arabs, of Muslims, and of humanity, and every person must resist it, to the best of his ability."*

2005 Hamas Website—Raed Said Hussein Saad: (Al-Qassam Brigade Commander) *"We succeeded, with Allah's grace, to raise an ideological generation that loves death like our enemies love life."*

2005 Palestinian TV: *"Annihilate the Infidels and the Polytheists. Your (God's) enemies and the enemies of the religion. God, count them and kill them to the last one, and don't leave even one."*

Raising a Generation of Jihadists: There are two types of schools in Islamic countries. There are public schools in which general subjects are taught as well as religious training. Then there are the **Madrasa, *(2)*** schools that place an emphasis on the Islamic religion. They are often boarding schools catering to children from poor families.

Although some general subjects are taught in Madrasas, the main emphasis is on the indoctrination of the student with the theology and practices of the Islamic religion. Arabic is taught so that the student can read and memorize the Koran. Most of these schools are supported by Saudi Arabia, particularly in Pakistan, where there are between 22,000 and 36,000 schools, depending on who is doing the counting. Many of these schools:

> *Teach jihad and hatred of infidels, especially America. . . . The leaders of the Afghanistan Taliban regime that harbored Osama bin Laden were all*

> *products of the Pakistan madrasas. . . . Pakistan madrasas have become a potent brewing pot for tens of thousands of Islamic militants who have spread conflict around the world from the Philippines to Indonesia to Russia to Central Asia to the World Trade Center in New York. (3)*

A 2008 US diplomatic cable expressed alarm that Saudi Arabian-financed madrasas were fostering *"religious radicalism"* in *"previously moderate regions of Pakistan"* as children from impoverished families were sent to isolated madrasas, and once there, often recruited for *"martyrdom operations."*

An interesting analysis of Islam was presented by the famous astrophysicist, philosopher, theologian, and Jesuit priest, Father Manual Carreia in an interview with **El Espanol**. He stated that *"Islam was created as decaffeinated Christianity because they simply have obscured what they did not understand in Christianity: One no longer talked about the Trinity, nor the incarnation of God for the simple reason that they had not understood it."* Therefore, Islam is a seventh to ninth-century developing form of *"a minimalist, distorted Christianity"* with its *"own distorted Christianity"* with its *"own theology,"* which is of *"very simple thinking."*

Carreia also added, *"I would say that Islam is the worst plague that humanity has seen in the past 2,000 years,"* and for Muslims, it is, therefore, *"impossible to respect human rights and the Western tradition."*

MARRAKESH DECLARATION

More than 250 Muslim religious leaders, heads of state, and scholars met on January 25–27, 2016 in Marrakesh, Morocco and formed a *"Declaration on the Rights of Religious Minorities in Predominately Muslim Majority Communities."* Representatives of persecuted religious communities were included in the conference. The Declaration declares:

Our firm commitment to the principles articulated in the Charter of Medina, whose provisions contained a number of the principles of constitutional contractual citizenship, such as freedom of movement, property ownership, mutual solidarity and defense, as well as principles of justice and equality before the law; and that the objectives of the Charter of Medina provide a suitable framework for national constitutions in countries with Muslim majorities, and the United Nations Charter and related documents, such as the Universal Declaration of Human Rights, are in harmony with the Charter of Medina, including consideration for public order.

NOTING FURTHER that deep reflection upon the various crises afflicting humanity underscores the inevitable and urgent need for cooperation among all religious groups, we AFFIRM HEREBY that such cooperation must be based on a 'Common Word,' requiring that such cooperation must go beyond mutual tolerance and respect, to providing full protection for the rights and liberties to all religious groups in a civilized manner that eschews coercion, bias, and arrogance.

BASED ON ALL OF THE ABOVE, we hereby:

Call upon Muslim scholars and intellectuals around the world to develop a jurisprudence of the concept of 'citizenship' which is inclusive of diverse groups. Such jurisprudence shall be rooted in Islamic tradition and principles and mindful of global changes.

Urge Muslim educational institutions and authorities to conduct a courageous review of educational curricula that addresses honestly and effectively any material that instigates aggression and extremism, leads to war and chaos, and results in the destruction of our shared societies;

Call upon politicians and decision makers to take the political and legal steps necessary to establish a constitutional contractual relationship among its citizens, and to support all formulations and initiatives that aim to fortify relations and understanding among the various religious groups in the Muslim World;

Call upon the educated, artistic, and creative members of our societies, as well as organizations of civil society, to establish a broad movement for the just treatment of religious minorities in Muslim countries and to raise awareness as to their rights, and to work together to ensure the success of these efforts.

Call upon the various religious groups bound by the same national fabric to address their mutual state of selective amnesia that blocks memories of centuries of joint and shared living on the same land; we call upon them to rebuild the past by reviving this tradition of conviviality, and restoring our shared trust that has been eroded by extremists using acts of terror and aggression;

Call upon representatives of the various religions, sects and denominations to confront all forms of religious bigotry, vilification, and denigration of what people hold sacred, as well as all speech that promote hatred and bigotry; AND FINALLY,

AFFIRM that it is unconscionable to employ religion for the purpose of aggressing upon the rights of religious minorities in Muslim countries."

Marrakesh
January 2016, 27ᵗʰ

What a wonderful declaration! But will it really be put into practice? One comment recorded in Wikipedia states:

> *The declaration has been widely welcomed, however commentators called for consistent legal and practical follow through of the sentiments expressed, not least in the country where the declaration was forged, which does not recognize its own indigenous Christians and persecutes and imprisons them, or in the birthplace of Islam, where there are reportedly many Saudi Christians, but which has been described by Voice of the Martyrs as 'one of the most oppressive nations in the world for Christians.'*

Ayman S. Ibrahim, a native of Egypt, is the **Bill and Connie Jenkins Assistant Professor of Islamic Studies** and senior fellow of the Jenkins Center for the Christian Understanding of Islam at the Southern Baptist Theological Seminary, has these remarks about the Declaration:

> *Will the governments of these countries allow Christians to build churches and freely worship in their faith and tradition? Will Christianity be recognized in Saudi Arabia? Will churches be built in Mecca, like mosques are being built in the West? Unofficial numbers tell of hundreds of thousands of Saudi converts to Christianity who cannot declare their convictions. Forget about building churches in Mecca; can Christians be allowed to enter Mecca?*

What about Northern Sudan? Can we expect a new era when Muslims are free to convert to any other religion? Minorities in Muslim-majority lands are tired of talking about religious equality. They are in desperate need of action.

The bad news is that this very Charter of Medina, upon which the Marrakesh Declaration is based, did not actually help religious minorities, particularly Jews, during Muhammad's time. Religious minorities during Muhammad's time were seized, expelled from their homes and often massacred. According to Muslim histories, one year after this charter was issued, Muhammad approached a Jewish tribe called Banu Qaynuqa and called for its members to convert to Islam. They refused. Muhammad then ordered a siege of the tribe, and fifteen days later, they surrendered and he expelled them from their home in Medina. Almost two years later, according to the renowned Muslim historian al-Tabari, the prophet expelled another Jewish tribe, named Banu al-Nadir. Was the charter in effect? What about the pluralistic community? Three years after the charter was signed, Muslim historians say, a third Jewish tribe, the Banu Qurayza, was massacred. Muhammad and his companions sieged the tribe for nearly twenty-five days, until its people surrendered. By decree, the men were killed, the property was divided, and the women and children were taken captive. It appears this earliest Muslim community struggled with religious pluralism. We should hope, and keep hoping for a better day. This declaration can do miracles if we, Arabs, do less talking, and begin to really apply religious freedom: no harassment, expulsion or executions of non-Muslim minorities, and freedom to choose one's faith. This, I pray, will be more than talk.

Yes, let us hope and pray that there will be a day when Muslims, Christians, Jews, and all other religions will really apply religious freedom in their communities and countries, where peace will be fostered and, as the prophet Isaiah said, **"They will beat their swords into plowshares and their spears into pruning hooks. Nation will not take up sword against nation, nor will they train for war anymore."** *(4)*

(1)   **From the film Obsession, 2006**
(2)   **Madrasa literally means "a place where learning and studying take place"**
(3)   **Ben Barber, The American Legion magazine, May 2002**
(4)   **Isaiah 2:4 (NIV)**

CONCLUSION

Having lived in Saudi Arabia for a short time; having visited Kuwait and Bahrain; having close relatives who are Muslim; and having studied, lectured, and taught classes on the Islamic religion for twenty-five years, I offer the following personal evaluation of Muslims and the Islamic religion.

The Muslim people of the Middle East (from Lebanon to Pakistan), can be very generous, loving, hospitable, and great friends, if they like you. On the other hand, if you do something that offends them, they can be vicious, vindictive, and vengeful. They can be your worse enemy. If you can "make amends," they can be forgiving.

Who was Muhammad? He was *not* a fictional character. I believe he was a very charismatic person. Although uneducated, he was highly intelligent, able to absorb and calculate what the situation or event called for and to put it into action. Before his religious experience, he would have been considered a very successful and outstanding businessman. In modern slang, we would say, "He could sell refrigerators to the Eskimos." He was able to absorb and then draw from the Jewish and Christian teachings and adapt them to form the basic Islamic religion.

After his flight to Medina from Mecca, Muhammad became a very successful politician and military general. Those he could not convert to Islam or dominate, he destroyed. Like many strong, autocratic leaders, he did not prepare anyone to follow in his footsteps, which resulted in divisions within Islam. After his death, Muhammad's life story was greatly enhanced by those who wanted to elevate their "prophet" to almost god-like status.

As Islam continued to expand and develop, there became no difference between religion and government. Islam's expansion came by war, incorporating the culture of the desert tribes of Arabia. The government *was* religion. There was no tolerance of other religions or any other form of government. The desert culture of male dominance was incorporated. In fact, much of the desert culture became the Islamic religion, along with the main tenant: monotheism . . . one God, Allah, and his prophet Muhammad. Along with Islamic rule was Islamic sharia law, the most restrictive and least democratic legal system in the world. (Many liken it to Nazism, Stalinism, and present-day North Korea.) According to Muslim leadership, peace will only come after all other religions submit to sharia law.

Jihad, with its two interpretations, still basically must be interpreted as "Holy War." Compromise can be secured in any war . . . temporarily, until the time when Islam has the largest majority or the strongest army or just wants to *take over*. Jihad is not "dead". It is alive and breeding in Africa, Palestine, Lebanon, Syria, Iraq, Iran, Saudi Arabia, Africa, Afghanistan, Pakistan, and the Philippines. It is alive on the internet and social media, recruiting from disillusioned, displaced, and naive people.

The Koran is technically poor. It is a collection of scattered ramblings with no coherent theme. Since it is written in "God's language" (*Arabic*), it has no value to the everyday Muslim, the majority of whom do not speak or understand Arabic. A Muslim may memorize and recite it, but does he really understand what it is saying when every fifth verse or so is incomprehensible? For example, it has none of the beauty of the Psalms, where the psalmist says, "*I have hidden your word in my heart that I might I might not sin against you.*" **(Psalm 119:11)**

The Crusades of the twelfth and thirteenth centuries continue to be considered an aggressive, bloodthirsty invasion of Christianity into peaceful Muslim lands, even by the President of United States. Raising this issue only displays ignorance of the history of the Islamic expansion that invaded and conquered the Holy Lands (Jerusalem) centuries before the Crusades (AD 636). The Christians wanted their holy sites in the former nation of Israel to be assessable to Christian Pilgrims and to be free of Muslim control and persecution. Their Crusades were to free the Holy Lands that had previously been conquered by the Muslims. The Muslims who were the invaders, not the Crusaders.

Islam has never progressed beyond the seventh century. It has remained frozen in time. However, there are Islamic scholars who do take risks in order to attempt to modernize Islamic theology and law. But they risk persecution, arrest, and even death. I believe the average Muslim just wants to have the freedom to practice his or her religion and to live the "good life." They are not jihadist or terrorists. They want to live in peace with their neighbors, whether they are Jewish, Christian, or atheist. The only problem is that they are the "silent majority."

Unfortunately, there are radical communities and national and international Muslim leaders whose rhetoric seeks to incite followers to take up arms against the "infidels" while the moderate Muslims remain silent and passive. Certainly it would be helpful if Muslim leadership would take bold steps to rein in the jihadists and reinterpret jihad as not a physical "Holy War" but a *Spiritual War* against poverty, ignorance, immorality, slavery (which still exists, particularly in Muslim countries), aggressive and hostile nations, and the evils that corrupt our communities, our nations, and our world order.

The danger posed by Islam is not that of the average Muslim but the practice of the doctrine of "political" Islam by radical Muslim leaders such as Ali Khamenei of Iran, Al-Shabab in Somali, Al- Qaeda and the Taliban in Afghanistan, and Mujao and Boko Haram in West Africa. Unfortunately, I do not see an end to the terrorism that plagues our present world until Islam undergoes a transformation in its ancient, corrupt, politicized, cultural religion.

If I were to define Islam in a few words, I would say that it is a systematic political body of concepts disguised as a religion.

Allah versus God: One of the major questions we need to ask is, "Do Christians and Muslims worship and serve the same God?" I have come to the conclusion that they do not worship the same God. In an interview with Carmel Communications, Cardinal Raymond Burke spoke to the issue, saying:

> *I don't believe it's true that we're all worshiping the same God, because the God of Islam is a governor. In other words, fundamentally. . . . Shira is their law, and that law, which comes from Allah, must dominate every man eventually. And it's not a law that's founded on love.*

Cardinal Burke emphasizes that,

> *. . . the church makes no pretense to govern the world, but rather that it's to inspire and assist those who govern the world to act justly and rightly toward the citizens.*

And,

> *. . . nothing has changed in the Islamic agenda from prior times in which our ancestors in the faith have had to fight to save Christianity. (1)*

Christians learned from the life of Jesus that God is love. Jesus said,

> *You have heard that it was said, "Love your neighbor and hate your enemy." But I tell you: Love your*

enemies and pray for those who persecute you, that
you may be sons of your Father in Heaven. (2)

Islam carries the law to the very extreme through sharia law. In St. Paul's letter to the church at Rome, he proclaims that we live under grace, not law.

But now, by dying to what once bound us, we have
been released from the law so that we serve in the
new way of the Spirit, and not the old way of written
code. (3)

The picture we have of the Islamic god (Allah) is that he is a god who speaks and listens only in Arabic; expects Muslims to rule the world through sharia law; tolerates and taxes non-Muslims who are monotheistic but forbids the building of worship centers for them; and destroys or enslaves all others (infidels).

This is not the God of Christians and Jews.

The Response of Many "Traditional" Mainline Christian Churches to Islam and jihad today is rather pathetic. They don't know enough about Islam to understand what motivates jihadists. The Church leadership has the same approach as the President of the United States who believes jihadists are only misguided or mentally ill terrorists with no connection to Islam. After all, they believe "Islam is a religion of Peace."

Most of the leadership in the United States denies that there is any serious problem, and if there is a problem, it is in the Middle East and does not have any effect on us, except for isolated incidents in New York City, Washington DC, or Orlando. According to the website *TheReligionofPeace.com (see: Index)* there have been 74 Islamic attacks in the United States from 1972 to June 6, 2016.

1972 to 2000 .... 27 Islamic terrorist
attacks—45 killed, 1,060 Injured

2001 to 2010 .... 29 Islamic terrorist attacks—3,035 killed, 383 Injured

2011 to 2016 (Jun. 6)... 18 Islamic terrorist attacks—90 killed, 338 Injured

William Kilpatrick, in his article in Crisis Magazine (Internet), points out how Pope Francis repeatedly assures us that Islamic violence is the work "*of a small group of fundamentalists*" who don't have anything to do with Islam, denying the inherently aggressive and violent nature of historic and present-day Islam.

Robert Spencer, in his recent column, stated: "*The Pope is betraying the Christians of the Middle East and the world, and all the victims of jihad violence, by repeating palpable falsehoods about the motivating ideology of attacks upon them.*"

It appears as though many Church leaders believe that these jihadists are not motivated by their religious belief system. Kilpatrick points out that millions of Christians in the Middle East and Africa are dead as a result of jihad violence, and millions more have been forced to flee their homes. The UN Refugee Agency (UNHCR) statistics show there are 21.3 million refugees, of which over half are under the age of eighteen:

- 54 percent come from Somalia, Afghanistan, and Syria.
- 33,972 people a day are forced to flee their homes because of conflict and persecution.
- An estimated 2 million were killed by Muslims in Sudan between 1983 and 1995.

Christians need to have a more realistic understanding of Islam, and this is why I have written this book.

(1) **"Why Christians and Muslims Worship Different Gods," article by Fr. Brandon O'Brien**
(2) **Matthew 5:43–45a NIV (3) Romans 7:6 NIV**

APPENDIX

Abdullah ibn Abul-Muttalib. Muhammad's father.

Abu Talib. Muhammad's uncle.

Ahmad. "To praise"; Muhammad's name that his mother received in a dream.

Aminah bint Wahb. Muhammad's mother. **Abd al-Muttalib.** Muhammad's grandfather. **Aisha.** Muhammad's child bride.

Al-Hajar al-Aswad. The Black Stone of the Kaaba.

Ali ibn Ali Tabib. Cousin and son-in-law of Muhammad.

Allah Akbar. "Allah is the greatest"; an expression of the Muslim faith.

Al-Buraq. "Lightening"; The white steed who carried Muhammad from Mecca to Jerusalem on the Night Journey to the Heavens and Jerusalem.

Al-Masjid an-Nabawi. "The Prophet's Mosque"; the second most important Mosque for Muslims located in Medina.

Ansar. "Helper"; the new converts to Islam in Medina.

Asahbiyya. "Tribal unity"; social solidarity

Bakkah. The former name of the city of Mecca, in Arabic, *Makka*. Located in the area known as Hejaz, in the Sirat Mountains, forty-five miles inland from the Red Sea.

Bahira. The Christian Monk who said he saw in Kunya (Muhammad) the markings of a prophet.

Bani Hashim Clan. Muhammad's clan.

Burka. Outer garment completely covering the body of women when in public.

Caliph. "Successor"; the person considered the religious successor to Muhammad.

Caliphate. An area or jurisdiction ruled by the Caliph.

Dhimma. "Protected person"; they were non-Muslims who were conquered by Muhammad's army. They had their rights fully protected in their communities, but, as citizens in the Islamic state, had certain restrictions. It was obligatory for them to pay the **jizyah** tax, which complemented the **zakat**, or Islamic tax, paid by the Muslim subjects. Dhimmis were excluded from specific duties assigned to Muslims and did not enjoy certain political rights reserved for Muslims, but they were otherwise equal under the laws of property, contract, and obligation.

Dhimmitude. "By their peaceful surrender to the Islamic army, they obtained the security for their life, belongings and religion, but they had to accept a condition of inferiority, spoliation and humiliation. As they were forbidden to possess weapons and give testimony against a Muslim, they were put in a position of vulnerability and humility." (Wikipedia)

Dhul al Hijjah. The twelfth month of the Islamic Calendar; the month of the Hajj.

Dijya. Blood money; financial compensation paid to the victim in cases of murder, bodily harm, or property damage.

Fatima. Muhammad's only surviving daughter to Khadijah, his first wife.

Fitnah. Upheaval or chaos.

Hadith. "Account" or "report"; the words, actions, and habits of the prophet.

Hajj. "To continually strive to reach one's goal"; the religious pilgrimage to Mecca and the religious acts required.

Halal. Foods that are permissible for Muslims to eat or drink under Islamic sharia law.

Hijrah. "Emigration"; Muhammad and his followers (fled) traveled from Mecca to Medina in AD 622. Their arrival became *day one* of the Islamic calendar.

Hudud. Punishments for breaking the sharia laws.

Ibrahim. "Abraham."

Id al-fitr. "Breaking of fast"; the feast at the end of Ramadan.

Iddah. The three-month waiting period (or three menstrual periods) for a marital divorce to be completed.

Ishmael's twelve sons. Nebaioth, Adbeel, Mibsam, Mishma, Mishma, Dumah, Massa, Hadad, Tema, Jetur, Naphish, Kedemah, Kedar

Ihram. "Purity" or "holiness"; of the rites of the Hajj **Islam.** "To surrender"; surrender to one God, Allah. **Jannah.** "Garden"; Paradise; Heaven(s)

Jihad. Consists of two phases: one is the inner spiritual struggle; the other is the outer physical struggle against the enemies of Islam.

Jizyah. The required tax on non-Muslims (Dhimma) living in Muslim-controlled territories. The tax is a per capita yearly tax on all adult, free, sane males while exempting women, children, elders, handicapped, the ill, the insane, monks, hermits, slaves, non-Muslim foreigners who only temporarily reside in Muslim lands, and those who chose to join military service, were exempt from payment, as were those who could not afford to pay.

Kaaba. "Cube"; the cubical building supposedly built by Abraham and Ishmael in Mecca. The building is 43 feet high with sides of 32.2 feet and 42.2 ft. in length. The inside floor is made of marble and limestone.

Khitan. Circumcision.

Kedar. One of Ishmael's sons. According to tradition, he is the ancestor of the Quraysh tribe, of which the prophet, Muhammad is a member.

Kunya. Another birth name of Muhammad.

Laelat al Miraj. Muhammad's night journey to the Heavens and Jerusalem.

Laylatul Qadr. The Night of Power.

Madrasa. Means literally, "a place where learning and studying take place."

Mahr. The dowry paid by the groom to the bride prior to the wedding.

Maghazi. Stories of military expeditions (particularly of Muhammad)

Maqam-e-Ibrahim. "The Station of Abraham"; the stone given by God when Abraham was rebuilding the Kaaba. **Masjid.** "A place of prostration"; Mosque. **Masjid al-Haran.** Mecca's Great Mosque.

Mihrab. Semicircular niche in the wall of the mosque indicating the direction of the Kaaba in Mecca.

Minbar. The pulpit where the imam (prayer leader) delivers his sermons in the mosque.

Minaret. The tower at the mosque that issues calls to prayers. Early mosques did not have minarets.

Mishaha. The prayer or worry beads used to recite the ninety-nine names of Allah.

Muezzin. The one who issues the calls to prayer from the minaret.

Muhajirum. Muslims who followed Muhammad from Mecca to Medina.

Muhammad. "The praised one"; the name bestowed upon Kunya after he placed the Black Stone in the Kaaba.

Muharram. The first month of the Islamic lunar calendar.

Musa. Moses.

Muslim. "One who submits to Allah"; one who follows the Islamic religion.

Musta'mins. Non-Muslim foreigners who only temporarily reside in Muslim lands. Those who chose to join military service were exempt.

Pbouh. Another birth name of Muhammad.

Qadi. "Decide"; the judge who reviews civil, judicial, and religious matters according to Islamic law.

Qiblah. "Direction"; the positon the Muslim assumes during prayers.

Qurahsh. Muhammad's tribe who were the protectors of the Kaaba.

Rakaat. Prayers during, following, and after circuits of the Kaaba during the Hajj.

Ramadan. "Scorching heat" or "dryness"; the ninth month of the Islamic Lunar Calendar (also the month of ritual fasting).

Ramal. The hurried pace around the Kaaba during the Hajj.

Ramy al-Jamart. "Stoning the Devil"; one of the rites of the Hajj.

Sa'ay. The walk or run of seven times between the two hills during the Hajj, another rite.

Salah. "Prayer."

Sadaqah. Voluntary charity giving.

Sawn. "To fast"

Semitic. People of the Middle East who belong to the same cultural and linguistic family (descendants of Shem, Noah's son). Inhabitants of the following modern countries are considered Semitic: Syria, Iraq, Jordon, Israel, Lebanon, Saudi Arabia, Yemen, Oman, Bahrain, Qatar, Egypt, United Arab Emirates, Northern Africa (Libya, etc.), and Kuwait. (*Note:* **Not** **Iran.**)

Sahn. The courtyard of the mosque.

Shadahah. "Testify" or "announce." "There is no God but Allah, and Muhammad is his prophet." This is the <u>first</u> of the Five Pillars of the Religion. Repeating this phrase in sincerity signifies a person's conversion to Islam.

Shaitan. "Satan."

Shiites. (Shiatn'Ali.) The party and followers of Ali ibn Ali Tabib, cousin and son-in-law of Muhammad.

Shura. "Consultation"; loosely considered to be an earlier form of Islamic democracy in the selection of the successor to Muhammad.

Sunnah. "Habit" or "usual practice"; The verbally transmitted record of the teaching, deeds, sayings, silent permissions, or disapprovals of Muhammad.

Sunni. (Derived from the phrase *Ahl-al-Sunnah* or "people of tradition.") Muslims whose lives are guided by four schools of legal thought, each of which strives to develop practical applications of the Sunnah.

Talaq. "Divorce"; "I divorce you" uttered three times by a husband legally completes a divorce.

Talbina. A meal of barley flower, milk, and honey.

Taqwa. The fear of God

Tawaf al-Wide. "To bid farewell"; The last circuit of the Kaaba at the end of the Hajj.

Tawaf. The circumambulation of the Kaaba in the Sacred Mosque in Mecca.

Ummah. "Community"; a collective community of Islamic people.

Wudu. Ritual "washing."

Wuquf. The sermon at the Sacred Mosque during the Hajj.

Yathrib. The former name of the city of Mecca.

Zahah. "To be made pure or just"; in Arabic, literally: "sweeting."

INDEX

OLD TESTAMENT NAMES FOR GOD

YHWH. "Lord"; (Exodus 4:10) The ancient Hebrew writings did not have vowels. The original Hebrew word was not vocalized because it was considered too sacred to pronounce. By the time vowels were introduced into their writings, the Hebrews had forgotten how to pronounce YHWH. When vowels were introduced, YHWH became YAHWEH. *(1)* In the sixteenth century, they substituted the vowels for Adonai, resulting in the name "Jehovah." This is the form of YHWH with "a," "o," and "a" (the vowels from Adonai, "my Lord") inserted between each consonant—Latinizing the word, changing the "Y" and "W" to "J" and "V."

YAHWEH. "Lord," meaning: He will be eternal; to exist and always will; unchangeable; the covenant-keeping God. This name is unique to God alone.

YAH/JAH. Lord (Psalm 68:4).

ADONAI. "Lord of Lords" occurs approximately 300 times in the Old Testament. The name Adonai, translated "Lord" (with only the letter "L" capitalized), occurs approximately 300 times in the Old Testament. No other name applied to God is more definite and more easily understood than this. Meaning to judge or rule, emphasizing God as Almighty Ruler and Covenant-keeper (Nehemiah 10:29; Psalms 109:21).

ADONAI-NISSI. The Lord, my banner or ensign (Exodus 17:15).

ADONAI-SHALOM. The Lord is our Peace (Judges 6:24).

CELA. Rock, stronghold, fortress, champion, *"Where I find safety."* (Psalms 18:2)

EHYEH-ASHER-EHYEH. "I AM that I AM." (Exodus 3:13–14)

EL. Lord God (Psalms 33:5).

ELOHIM. One of the most prevalent Hebrew words for God, used more than 2,500 times in the Old Testament; meaning the God who is strong and mighty and the object of fear; emphasizing God as Creator, governing and redeeming mankind; also, God's direct connection with the nation of Israel (Genesis 2:4).

EL GMULOT. The God on Retribution (Jeremiah 51:56).

EL JIRETH. The Lord will provide (Genesis 22:13–14).

EL MAKEH. The Lord smites and punishes sin (Ezekiel 7:9).

EL MEKADDISHKEM. The Lord Sanctifier (Leviticus 20:7–8).

EL OLAM. Everlasting God. Olam means "age" or "hidden" (Isaiah 40:28).

EL QANNA. A jealous God, if Israel follows other gods, i.e., Molock, Baal, etc., (Exodus 20:5).

EL RAPHA. The Lord who heals (Psalms 103:3).

EL ROI. The God of sight who keeps watch . . . "the Lord is my Shepherd" (Genesis 16:3; Psalms 23).

EL SABOATH. The Lord of hosts; angelic armies (1 Samuel 1:3).

EL SHADDAI. God Almighty . . . to be powerful; nourishing; and sustainer (Genesis 17:1).

EL SHAMMAH. The Lord is present (Ezekiel 48:35).

EL TSIDKENU. The Lord our Vindication; Righteousness (Jeremiah 23:6). *(2)*

(1) **Centuries later, scholars Latinized the word to "Jehovah."**
(2) **Translators are not sure whether to translate this word "Vindication" or "Righteousness."**

TITLES IN NEW TESTAMENT OF THE TRINITARIAN GOD

(Compiled by Loren Jacobs)

Father: Matthew 6:9	**Abba ("Daddy")**: Romans 8:15
God The Father: 2 Timothy 1:2	**Father Of Our Lord Yeshua The Messiah**: Colossians 1:3
The Father Of Lights: James 1:17	**The Father Of Glory**: Ephesians 1:17
The Father Of Spirits: Hebrews 12:9	**Father of Mercies**: 2 Corinthians 1:3
God (Elohim): 2 Corinthians 9:7	**The God Of Our Fathers (Elohay Avotaynu)**: Acts 7:32
The God Of Abraham, Isaac And Jacob: Acts 7:32	**God Of All**: 2 Corinthians 1:3
God Of Peace (Elohay Shalom): Hebrews 13:20	**The God Of Glory (Elohay Kavod)**: Acts 7:2
The Living God (Elohay Chaiyim): 2 Corinthians 3:3, 6:16	**The God Of Israel (Elohay Yisrael)**: Matthew 15:31
Lord God (YHVH Elohim): Acts 3:22	**Lord God of Israel (YHVH Elohay Yisrael)**: Luke 1:68
Lord Almighty (YHVH Shaddai): 2 Corinthians 6:18	**The Almighty (Shaddai)**: Revelation 1:8
Power (Ha Gevurah): Mark 14:62	**The Creator (HaBoray)**: Romans 1:25, 1 Peter 4:19

The Most High God: Hebrews 7:1	**The Divine Nature:** Romans 1:20, 2 Peter 1:4
Lord Of Armies: James 5:4	**The Majestic Glory:** 2 Peter 1:17
The Majesty: Hebrews 1:3	**The King Of The Nations:** Revelation 15:3
The Lawgiver And Judge: James 4:12	**The Eternal Immortal Invisible King:** 1 Timothy 1:17
Sovereign: 1 Timothy 6:15	**Heaven:** Matthew 21:25
A Consuming Fire: Hebrews 12:29	

NEW TESTAMENT NAMES FOR JESUS

(Compiled by Loren Jacobs)

Yeshua Of Nazareth: Matthew 26:71	**Messiah:** John 1:41
The Son: John 8:36	**Only Begotten Son:** 1 John 4:9
Beloved Son: Matthew 3:17	**Son Of David:** Matthew 1:1
The Root And Offspring Of David: Revelation 22:16	**Son Of Abraham:** Matthew 1:1
Abraham's Seed: Galatians 3:16	**Son Of Joseph:** John 1:45
Son Of Man: Matthew 26:64, (see Daniel 7:13)	**Son Of God:** Matthew 26:63
Son of the Father: 2 John 1:3	**Son Of The Most High:** Luke 1:32
Only Begotten God: John 1:18	**Firstborn:** Hebrews 1:6
Firstborn Of All Creation: Colossians 1:15	**Beginning Of The Creation Of God:** Revelation 3:14
Firstborn From The Dead: Revelation 1:5	**The Last Adam:** 1 Corinthians 15:45
Rabbi ("Teacher"): Matthew 23:8	**King Of Israel:** Mark 15:32
King Of The Jews: Matthew 27:37	**The Word:** John 1:1
The Word Of God: Revelation 19:13	**The Word Of Life:** 1 John 1:1
The Life: John 11:25	**I AM:** John 8:58 (see Exodus 3:14)
Lord: Romans 10:9–13 (see Joel 2:32)	**God:** John 1:1
The Man: (John 19:5)	**Immanuel ("God with Us"):** Matthew 1:23
Master ("Chief," "Commander"): Luke 8:24	**The Expected One:** Luke 7:19
Savior Of The World: John 4:42	**Savior Of All Men:** 1 Timothy 4:10
The Deliverer: Romans 11:26	**The Prophet:** John 1:25 (see Deuteronomy 18:15)

Holy One: Acts 3:14	**Righteous One**: Acts 3:14
Prince: Acts 5:31	**Prince Of Life**: Acts 3:15
Living One: Luke 24:5	**Judge Of The Living And The Dead**: Acts 10:42
Stone: Mark 12:10	**Chief Cornerstone**: Mark 12:10
Chief Shepherd: 1 Peter 5:4	**Good Shepherd**: John 10:11
Shepherd And Guardian Of Our Souls: 1 Peter 2:25	**The Lamb**: Revelation 5:12

Passover Lamb: 1 Corinthians 5:7	**Lamb of God**: John 1:36
Lion Of Judah: Revelation 5:5	**Advocate ("Counsel For The Defense")**: 1 John 2:1
Light Of The World: John 8:12	**King Of Kings And Lord Of Lords**: Revelation 19:16
The Faithful Witness: Revelation 1:5	**The Faithful And True One**: Revelation 19:11
The Amen: Revelation 3:14	**Servant**: Acts 4:27
The Bright Morning Star: Revelation 22:16	**Sunrise From On High**: Luke 1:78
The Apostle: Hebrews 3:1	**The Great High Priest**: Hebrews 4:14
The Author And Perfecter Of Faith: Hebrews 12:2	**The Chosen One**: Luke 9:35
The Mediator: 1 Timothy 2:5	**The Way, The Truth, And The Life**: John 14:6
The Door: John 10:7	**The Alpha And The Omega**: Revelation 22:13
The First And The Last: Revelation 22:13	**The Beginning And The End**: Revelation 22:13
The Head Of The Body, The Church: Colossians 1:18	**Head Over All Things**: Ephesians 1:22
Heir Of All Things: Hebrews 1:2	**The Image Of The Invisible God**: Colossians 1:15
God's Mystery: Colossians 2:2	**Horn Of Salvation**: Luke 1:69
The Power Of God: 1 Corinthians 1:24	**The Wisdom Of God**: 1 Corinthians 1:24
The Beloved: Matthew 12:18	**The Bridegroom**: John 3:29
The Bread Of God: John 6:33	**The Bread Out Of Heaven**: John 6:32
The Bread Of Life: John 6:35	**The True Vine**: John 15:1
The Vinedresser: John 15:1	**The Resurrection**: John 11:25

NEW TESTAMENT NAMES FOR THE HOLY SPIRIT

(Compiled by Loren Jacobs)

The Spirit: Romans 2:29	**The Holy Spirit**: Luke 3:16
The Holy Spirit of God: Ephesians 4:30	**The Holy Spirit Of Promise**: Ephesians 1:13
The Spirit of the Living God: 2 Corinthians 3:3	**The Spirit Of The Lord**: Luke 4:18
The Eternal Spirit: Hebrews 9:14	**The Spirit Of Truth**: John 15:26
The Spirit Of Yeshua: Acts 16:7	**The Spirit Of Yeshua The Messiah**: Philippians 1:19
The Spirit Of Messiah: Romans 8:9	**The Spirit Of God**: Romans 8:9
Helper or Comforter: John 14:26	

The Holy Spirit is Compared to:

Clothing: (Luke 24:49) Because He clothes us with power from on high.	**A Dove:** (Matthew 3:16) Because the dove is a symbol of purity and peace, flies in the heavens, and was used as a sacrifice for the poor.
A Pledge: (2 Corinthians 1:22) Because He is the pledge and the down payment of our inheritance.	**A Seal:** (Ephesians 1:13) Because a seal protects, makes secure, and demonstrates ownership.
Fire: (Acts 2:3): Because fire separates the impure from the pure; it cleanses and purifies.	**Oil:** (Acts 10:38) Because oil was used for anointing, for healing, and nourishment, and was burned to give light.
Water: (John 7:38) Because water is simple yet mysterious. It is tasteless, formless, colorless, transparent, and buoyant. It can hold up a huge ship. It is used for transportation. The Holy Spirit holds us up and transports us through this world to the World To Come. Water cleanses and refreshes. With water, there is life, growth, and fruitfulness. Without water, there are deserts.	**Wind:** (John 3:8) Because we can't see the wind, but we can see its results. Just as the winds blows wherever it wants, so God's Spirit is sovereign. He gives gifts as He wills. The wind can be powerful like a tornado or hurricane, or it can be a cool, refreshing breeze.
Breath: (John 20:22) Because without breath, we die. God's Breath gives us life. We have life and intimacy with God due to His indwelling Spirit.	**Wine:** (Ephesians 5:18) Because we are not to be drunk with wine but be filled with the Spirit.

THE NINETY-NINE NAMES OF ALLAH

Name Meaning Name Meaning Name Meaning

Name	Meaning	Name	Meaning	Name	Meaning
Allah	God	Al'Azim	The Mighty	Al Rahman	The Compassionate
Al Ghafur	The Forgiving	Ash Shakur	The Grateful	Al Rahim	The Merciful
Al Malik	The King	Al 'Ali	The Lofty	Al Quddus	The Holy
As Salam	The Peace	Al Kabir	The Great	Al Mu'min	The One with Faith
Al Hafiz	The Guardian	Al Muhaymin	The Protector	Al Muqit	The Nourisher
Al 'Aziz	The Mighty	Al Hasib	The Reckoner	Al Jabbar	The Repairer
Al Jalil	The Majestic	Al Mutakabbir	The Imperious	Al Karim	The Generous
Al Khaliq	The Creator	Ar Raqib	The Watcher	Al Bari'	The Maker
Al Mujib	The Responder	Al Musawwir	The Fashioner	Al Wasi'	The All-Sufficient
Al Ghaffar	The Forgiver	Al Hakim	The Wise	Al Qahhar	The Dominant
Al Wadud	The Loving	Al Wahhab	The Bestower	Al Majid	The Glorious
Al Razzaq	The Provider	Al Ba'ith	The Resurrector	Al Fattah	The Opener
Ash Shahid	The Witness	Al 'Alim	The Knower	Al Haqq	The Truth
Al Qaibid	The Contractor	Al Wakil	The Trustee	Al Basit	The Expander
Al Qawi	The Strong	Al Khafid	The Humbler	Al Matin	The Firm
Al Rafi'	The Exalter	Al Wali	The Friend	Al Mu'izz	The Honorer
Al Hamid	The Praiseworthy	Al Mudhill	The Abaser	Al Muhsi	The Counter
Al Mubdi'	The Originator	As Sami'	The Hearer	Al Mu'id	The Restorer
Al Basir	The Seer	Al Muhyi	The Life-Giver	Al Hakam	The Judge
Al Mumit	The Death-Giver	Al 'Adl	The Just	Al Hayy	The Living
Al Laif	The Subtle	Al Quayyum	The Self-Subsistant	Al Khabir	The Awarer
Al Wajid	The Finder	Al Halim	The Gentle	Al Majid	The Noble
Al Ahad	The One	As Samad	The Eternal	Al Qadir	The Abler
Al Muqtadir	The Powerful	Al Muqaddim	The Expediter	Al Mu'akhkir	The Deferrer
Al Awwal	The First	Al Khir	The Last	Az Zahir	The Manifest
Al Batin	The Hidden	Al Wali	The Governor	Al Barr	The Benefactor

Al Muntaqim	The Avenger	Al 'Afuw	The Pardoner	Ar A'uf	The Compassionate
Al Muqsit	The Equitable	Al Jami'	The Gatherer	Al Ghani	The Self- Sufficient
Al Mughni	The Enricher	Al Mani	The Preventer	Ad Darr	The Distresser
An Nafi'	The Benefactor	An Nur	The Light	Al Hadi	The Guide
Al Badi	The Incomparable	Al Baqi	The Enduring	Al Warith	The Inheritor
Ar Rashid	The Rightly Guided	As Sabur	The Patient	Al Muta'ali	The Exalted
At Tawwab	The Acceptor of Repentance				
Malik al-Mulk	The Ruler of the Kingdom				
Dhu 'i-Jalal Wa 'l-Ikram	Lord of Majesty and Generosity				

ARAB CLOTHING

The **abaya** or "cloak" is sometimes also called an *aba*. It is a simple, loose overgarment, essentially a robe-like dress, worn by some women in parts of the Muslim world including North Africa and the Arabian Peninsula. Traditional *abayat* are black and may be either a large square of fabric draped from the shoulders or head or a long caftan. The *abaya* covers the whole body except the head, feet, and hands. It can be worn with the *niqab*, a face veil covering all but the eyes. Some women also wear long, black gloves so their hands are covered as well.

A **niqab** or "veil" (also called a *ruband*) is a cloth that covers the face as a part of sartorial hijab. It is worn by some Muslim women in public areas and in front of non-mahram men, especially in the Hanbali Muslim faith tradition. The niqab is worn in the Arab countries of the Arabian Peninsula such as Saudi Arabia, Yemen, Oman, and the United Arab Emirates.

A **burka** is an enveloping outer garment worn by women in some Islamic traditions to cover their bodies when in public. The face- veiling portion is usually a rectangular piece of semi-transparent cloth with its top edge attached to a portion of the head-scarf so that the veil hangs down, covering the face, and can be turned up if the woman prefers. In other styles, the niqab is attached by one side and covers the face only below the eyes, allowing the eyes to be seen.

The **agal** or "bond" or "rope" is an accessory worn usually by Arab men. It is a black cord, worn doubled and used to keep the ghutrah or *kufiya* in place on the wearer's head.

The **kufiya** (meaning "from the city of Kufa" in Arabic) is typically worn by Arabs, as well as by some Jews and Kurds. It is commonly found in arid regions, as it provides protection from sunburn, dust, and sand. Its distinctive, standard woven checkered pattern may have originated in an ancient Mesopotamia.

The **thobe** (*thawb*) is an ankle-length Arab garment, usually with long sleeves, similar to a robe. It is commonly worn in the Arabian Peninsula, Iraq, and neighboring Arab countries.

A **bisht** is a traditional men's cloak popular in Arabia and some Arab countries. The garment and its name originated in Persia. It is essentially a flowing outer cloak made of wool and worn over the thobe. Unlike the thobe, it is usually black, brown, beige, cream, or gray in color. As winters are warm in this region, the bisht is usually only worn for prestige on special occasions such as weddings or festivals such as Eid or for Friday prayer. In Iraq, it is worn by tribal chiefs. In Saudi Arabia, the high-quality bisht is made of camel hair.

A **hijab** is a veil traditionally worn by Muslim women in the presence of adult males outside of their immediate family, which usually covers the head and chest. The term can further refer to any head, face, or body covering worn by Muslim women that conforms to a certain standard of modesty. Hijab can also be used to refer to the seclusion of women from men in the public sphere, or it may denote a metaphysical dimension, for example, referring to "the veil which separates man or the world from God."

A **shayla** is a piece of Islamic headgear worn by women. It is usually a black mask and is considered a form of a hijab in the form of a half niqab with part of the face still visible. It is traditionally worn by some women in Saudi Arabia and the Gulf.

RESOURCES

Ali, A. Yusuf, trans. The Holy Qur'an (Arabic text & English translation), 1983.

Ali, Maulana Muhammad. The Muslim Prayer-Book, Reprint: 1998.

Barber, Ben. The American Legion Magazine, May 2002. Belyaev, E.A. Arabs, Islam and the Arab Caliphian in Early Middle Ages, 1969.

Booker, Richard. Radical Islam's War Against the West, 2006. Buchhart, Johann L. Travels in Arabia, 1829.

Cleary, Thomas. The Essential Koran, 1998. Davis, Gregory M. Religion of Peace? 2006.

Emerick, Yahiya. Complete Idiot's Guide to Understanding Islam, 2002.

Farah, Caesar E. Islam, 2000.

Hamada, Louis Babjat. Understanding the Arab World, Author, 1990.

Hisham ibn al-Kalbi. Book of Idols, (737–819) (This book no longer in print.)

Karsh, Efraim. Islamic Imperialism, 2008.

Lester, Toby. "What is the Koran?" The Atlantic Monthly, January 1999.

Obsession. Directed by Wayne Kopping. 2005. Washington, D.C.: Clarion Project, 2006. DVD.

Rodwell, J.M., trans. The Koran (English translation), 1994.

Rushdie, Salman. NY Times, Nov 2, 2001.

Sfar, Mondher. In Search for the Original Koran, 2008.

Shakir, M.H., trans. The Qur'an (Arabic text & English translation), 1997.

Shakir, M.H., trans. The Qur'an (Arabic text & English translation), 1999.

Spencer, Robert. The Politically Incorrect Guide to Islam, 1962. Spencer, Robert. The Truth About Muhammad, 2007, Printing 2015.

The Holy Bible. The New International Version, 1986.

The Human Rights Watch and United States Religious Freedom Report

The New English Bible with Apocrypha, 1970.

The United Nations Declaration of Human Rights Report

Torah, Nevi'm, and Kethuvim. TANAKH The Holy Scriptures, 1985.

Warraq, Ibn, editor. The Origins of the Koran, 1998.

Warraq, Ibn. The Quest for the Historical Muhammad, 2000. Warraq, Ibn. What the Koran Really Says, 2002.

Warraq, Ibn. Why I am Not a Muslim, 1995.

Weiss, Walter M. ISLAM: An illustrated historical overview, 2000.

Williams, John Alders. Islam, 1962.

Ye'or, Bat. The Decline of Eastern Christianity Islam, 1996.

OTHER RESOURCES

Jan Michael Otto

Dr. Brian M. English

Dr. Peter Hammond

Dr. Bruce Frohnen

Dr. Thomas Madden

Dr. Riley-Smith

Bernard Lewis

Matt Slick

Javed Ahmad Ghamidi

Lincoln Clapper

Robert Spencer

Ignaz Goldzicher

R. Stephen Humphrey

Ibu Al-Rawandi

Ayman S. Ibrahim

Crone & Cook

Helmi Faisal

William Kilpatrick, Crisis Magazine

The Rev. Dr. Manuel Carreia, El Espanol Wikipedia

<u>Thomas King</u>: (January 16, 2016)

St. John of Damascus

Abo, The Perfumer of Bagdad

St. Francis of Assisi

St. Gregory Palamas

Martin Luther: War Against the Turks

John Calvin: Larger Catechism (1643)

   Directory for the Public Worship of God

   Dutch Dordt Bible (1637)

   Institutes

   Sermons on Timothy and Titus

   Commentary on Second Thessalonians

<u>**Marrakesh Declaration:**</u> (January 25–27, 2016)

"The Declaration of the Rights of Religious Minorities In

Predominately Muslim Majority Communities"

<u>**The Jakarta Summit:**</u> (May 9, 2016)

A. Mustofa Bisri, Spiritual Leader

Jusuf Kalla, Vice President of Indonesia

Nico Prucha, Research Fellow at London's King's College

Azyumaradi Azra, Islam Scholar

Fazal Ghani Kahar, Founder of Afghanistan's Islam Nusantara

Dr. KH Said Aquil Siradj, Chairman of Nahdlatul Ulama (NU)

Printed in the United States
By Bookmasters